2020 VISIONS

2020 VISIONS

The Futures of Canadian Education

CRAWFORD KILIAN

ARSENAL PULP PRESS
VANCOUVER

2020 VISIONS

Copyright © 1995 by Crawford Kilian

ARSENAL PULP PRESS
100-1062 Homer Street
Vancouver, B.C.
Canada V6B 2W9

The publisher gratefully acknowledges the assistance of the
Canada Council and the Cultural Services Branch, B.C.
Ministry of Small Business, Tourism and Culture.

Printed and bound in Canada

CANADIAN CATALOGUING IN PUBLICATION DATA:
Kilian, Crawford, 1941-
   2020 visions

   Includes index.
   ISBN 1-55152-016-8

   1. Education and state—British Columbia. 2. Community
and school—British Columbia. 3. Education—Canada. I.
Title. II. Title: Twenty-twenty visions.
LC91.2.B7K544 1995   379.711   C95-910231-0

Contents

In 1988, I wrote an admiring review of Northrop Frye's book *On Education*. He sent me a note of thanks in which he observed: "I only wish you were not so utterly right about the situation being essentially unchanged since the fifties."

As a scholar, teacher, and citizen, he inspired generations of students. Through his books, he reached thousands, like me, who never met him but considered him a mentor. I dedicate this book to his memory.

Introduction

Let's start with the day I really got scared about education.

It didn't happen because a student pulled a knife on me, or another student displayed ignorance on an astronomical scale. It didn't happen when my departmental budget took a cut, or my classes got bigger.

It happened on the morning of March 11, 1993 when I took part in a panel for senior British Columbia school administrators.

The session's title, appropriately but ominously, was "Public Confidence in Restructuring Education." It was part of the annual general meeting of the B.C. School Superintendents' Association; the supers had invited me, as education columnist for the Vancouver *Province*, to offer some advice on building public confidence by maintaining good media relations in a time when the schools were under increasing fire.

Planning for the panel had been extensive: I had even been part of an international conference call including the panelists, the keynote speaker in the United States, and the Minister of Education herself, Anita Hagen. So I went into the conference feeling pretty comfortable about what I was going to say.

The conference was in the Pan Pacific Hotel, a spectacular and palatial setting overlooking Vancouver's harbour; the supers had a floor of the convention area. Several of them greeted me warmly when I arrived. One apologized for the relatively light turnout; with so many school districts facing teacher strikes, he explained, many administrators had been unable to make it.

Still, an impressive assembly of middle-aged men in suits (with a few well-tailored women) gathered in a beautiful room to hear our panel: the head of the B.C. Federation of Parents' Advisory Councils; a businessman with long experience in education; and me, a college teacher, education writer, and former school trustee.

Following our presentations, Anita Hagen and her deputy minister were among those who responded. As I listened to Hagen, I began to feel uneasy. She was dealing in clichés and truisms. "This government is dedicated to educating all children," was about as dramatic as she got. It seemed like pretty thin stuff for the province's top educators.

Afterward, several supers congratulated me on my comments (another collection of truisms, I confess) and observed without prompting that the panel had been an excellent part of a worthwhile meeting. One thanked me and added with a nervous grin: "I thought you went pretty easy on us."

Heading back to work at Capilano College, I realized how right he was. I had just attended a conference with the top people in B.C. education, people overseeing the education of half a million children and the jobs of fifty thousand or more teachers and support staff. They were all highly educated, highly experienced, very highly paid men and women. While the system coughed and shuddered and stopped outright in some places, they had traveled at taxpayers' expense to a very costly hotel. (Three administrators from suburban Surrey, thirty minutes' drive away, were running up sizable room bills that would later get them in trouble when the public found out.) There they had sat in quiet, attentive rows like star pupils, while we'd spoonfed them cold pablum—and they'd *loved* it!

That was what scared me. The leaders of the public schools, from the minister herself on down to the humblest assistant super of some remote district, were terminally out of touch with their own system and the communities that supported it. This had happened, furthermore, after more than a decade of political conflict over the B.C. schools; anyone who'd gone through that dark age should have developed some sense of reality. Far from helping them, I'd only contributed to their isolation.

What I should have told them was to leave the Pan Pacific Hotel at once, to deny they had ever been there, and to stay at their desks as long as it took to resolve their local and provincial problems. The last thing a bureaucrat needs, when the bureaucracy is dying, is a weekend in a good hotel pretending to become a better bureaucrat.

The more I have learned about education, the more I have come to respect the people who work in it. But I believe the system of North American public and post-secondary education, to which hundreds of thousands of us have given our working lives, is ready for dismantling.

Not that the system has utterly failed. Parts of it, like the curate's egg, are quite good. But as a society we have outgrown it; as an economy we cannot afford it; as individuals we do not often find what we need in it. As educators, we are failing to meet both our students' needs and our own.

The crisis in education is really a crisis of the education bureaucracy. Put some students and a teacher in any clean, well-lighted Canadian place and some extremely good teaching and learning will likely occur. But the costs of arranging such an encounter are rising daily. Worse yet, they are rising beyond the desire of taxpayers to pay them. Both teachers and students are changing; responding to those changes strains the bureaucracy. And ultimately the bureaucracy looks after its own interests, not those of the students it says it serves.

Most critics of the system understand that much, but their calls for reform are beside the point. Dropout rates will not improve if we turn parents into deputy bureaucrats and drag them into endless committee meetings for consultation. Students will not do better on international exams if we streamline the administrative hierarchy, merge school districts, or cut back on the photocopying budget. Changing the textbooks and the way we use them will not create sublimely literate young people. The system will not perform better if we smack bureaucrats on the hand with a ruler and cut their salaries.

Least of all will students do better with a change of bureaucrats. Education's private sector has just as many charlatans, ideologues, and timeservers as the public schools, and they are quite prepared to offer whatever pretence of schooling will attract paying parents.

The people in charge of the system—the trustees, senior administrators, teachers' union executives, provincial government bureaucrats—are smart, capable, well-informed men and women. They know a hell of a lot more about the schools than most of their critics, and they probably care more. But they behave like Charlie Chaplin in *Modern Times*—so programmed in thought and behaviour that even when the machine sucks them in and grinds them between its cogs, they keep tightening bolts and trying to keep the machine running.

For them, the crisis in education is a fuel shortage: They don't have the money they need to pay for all the programs, personnel, buildings, vehicles and furniture that education seems to require. Resolving the crisis has nothing to do with real educational results, but with the political consequences of horizontal versus vertical cuts—of starving the whole system, or amputating parts of it for the good of the rest.

You can't really blame the bureaucrats for their attitude. Their daily reality is one of jobs, payrolls, and power. Cut their budgets and they lose valued employees, freedom of choice, and power. Somewhat more abstractly, bureaucrats also realize they're not serving children as well as they otherwise could, but children aren't very significant in the daily working lives of senior educators. (Kilian's Third Law predicts that status in education will be inversely proportional to the age of one's students and the time spent teaching them. So primary teachers, who deal with small children all day long, have the least status despite their obvious and paramount importance in the system. University presidents enjoy the most status because they don't teach at all, and the people they don't teach are adults.)

Faced with a fuel shortage, educators try to figure out how to improve their mileage, or how to take shorter trips with fewer passengers. The one option they never consider is junking their poor old beater and finding another way to get to work.

This book is an attempt to consider some of the attitudes that have brought public education to this sorry state, and to examine our choices for the future. It is not an attempt to change your mind and bring you around to my version of reality. As I'll try to show in the first chapter, our differences about education spring from sharply conflicting visions of the way the world works and the power that people can exert over that world. If my arguments persuade you only that your own views are far wiser than mine, well and good. And if you agree with my premises but come to far different conclusions, that's fine with me. As a public institution, education is an inevitable compromise among constantly changing agendas. That is as it should be in a democracy. All I hope is that I can give you a useful new perspective.

In the last decade, I've learned that an education system, even of a small Canadian province, is too big and complex for any one person to comprehend. But what's happening here in B.C. appears to be happening in other places as well: the rest of Canada, the United States, the industrial nations of Europe. Some are behind us, others ahead, but we are all facing a major test of the system. So while many of my examples and arguments come from my own experience and that of my province, I don't think I'll be offering only anecdotal evidence from an atypical area.

The question is not whether the system will survive—it will not. The question is: what will replace the present system, and what kind of society will the new system both reflect and help to create?

1

Caution and Confidence:
Conflicting Visions in Education

In my 1985 book *School Wars*, I argued a conflict between
two social groups: schismatics and ecumenicals. Schismatics, I contended, lacked much interest in social responsibility; they wanted simply to maximize their own benefits,
without caring what happened to others. Ecumenicals, by
contrast, wanted to bring everyone—especially those on the
social margins—into full and equal participation in society.
I blamed the Social Credit government of British Columbia
in the early 1980s for supporting the schismatics, starving
the public schools, and subsidizing the private system. I
found the New Democratic Party much more in tune with
the ecumenical ideal, and imagined it would foster that
ideal in education.

Live and learn. Almost a decade later, the New Democrats in power have played the same political games with
education that the Socreds did, and in this they're no different from any other government in North America.

I don't really blame those governments. They're trying
to reconcile two deeply opposed concepts about the world
and the way people should behave. While it's easy to see
the opponents battling on many fronts, I hadn't realized
just how deep the divisions go, or how old and complex

they are, until I recently ran across a book published in 1987 by an American economist.

Thomas Sowell's *A Conflict of Visions* is a book important enough to deserve rescue from itself. His tight control of subject and language, and his deliberately abstract style, sometimes make Sowell his own worst enemy. His views deserve wide dissemination and discussion, yet he himself presents them in a manner accessible to only a handful. When he smells smoke in a crowded theater, his response is to whisper: "Combustion appears to be occurring in the venue of this dramatic presentation."

Sowell brilliantly outlines "constrained" and "unconstrained" visions of the way the world works. He confines himself very closely to a few key topics where those visions have had an impact—economics and law in particular. His examples tend to be quotations from a handful of thinkers including William Godwin, Adam Smith, Karl Marx, Friedrich Hayek, and Milton Friedman. He rarely cites events inspired by one vision or the other. Surprisingly, he pays very little attention to the means by which these thinkers' visions originate and propagate themselves. How a vision arises, and how it appeals to some people but not to others, are outside Sowell's scope; yet hundreds of millions have fought, suffered, and died in the name of these visions. While he subtitles his book "Ideological Origins of Political Struggles," the struggles might all be happening over sherry at the faculty club.

At the risk, therefore, of doing violence to the fine detail of Sowell's argument, I want to show how his ideas relate to North American education, which has been a major vehicle for the spread of visions. But I will do so with somewhat different terminology.

A key obstacle to applying Sowell's ideas is his basic vocabulary. "Constrained" and "unconstrained" visions are simply inadequate terms; he uses them constantly, and each time the reader must pause to recall their definitions.

While they are semantically fairly neutral, one is a negative of the other; both are clumsy. At least one sympathetic reviewer of the book observed that better terms must be available, and indeed they are.

In discussing Sowell's ideas, therefore, I will replace the constrained vision with the *cautious* vision, one that springs from a keen awareness of the limits on individual human knowledge and power. And I will call the unconstrained vision the *confident* vision, buoyed up by a sense of what humans—individually and collectively—can achieve. I hope these terms reflect the virtue that each vision can embody, while implying the vice that each can foster.

Caution, then, springs from our experience with our own limitations throughout history: our ignorance, our selfishness, our pigheadedness. With each advance in knowledge, caution also learns how much more we still don't know. The cautious vision sees no one much brighter than the most stupid, and no one much better than the worst. Caution expects any human enterprise to get into trouble, and it expects no rescue from the supernatural.

The cautious vision recognizes the reality of social benefits: a peaceful community, an educated citizenry. It sees those benefits as arising from tradeoffs and the unintended consequences of individuals seeking their own good and not that of society. So students go to school to qualify for good jobs and the chance to make money; if they must pay higher taxes on their resulting incomes, that is a tradeoff presumably worth making. From a cautious government's point of view, subsidizing students' education is itself a worthwhile tradeoff if the investment of tax revenues in schools leads to higher tax revenue that it can plow into still further investments. If a well-educated society can also afford to defend itself, expand its markets, and support its weaker members, those are side effects of students' self-centered efforts to enrich themselves.

The cautious vision respects specialized knowledge and

the expertise it brings, but it does not assume that expertise in one field implies expertise in others. An oncologist may predict, with great accuracy, the life expectancy of a woman with terminal lung cancer; that same oncologist may be sadly misguided in predicting that an advertising campaign will discourage girls from taking up smoking, and thereby reduce future lung-cancer fatalities. Still less will the cautious vision respect the oncologist's prediction about the best outcome of a trade dispute or how children will most effectively learn to read. And the cautious vision will be very reluctant to grant the oncologist, or any other specialist, the power to decide on trade issues or classroom teaching strategies.

The confident vision, by contrast, sees human nature as indefinitely perfectible, capable of creating social benefits out of internal disposition rather than external incentive. Instead of seeking *tradeoffs* to mitigate permanent conditions, it seeks solutions to problems that are sure to vanish when reason and knowledge go to work on them. And it seeks those solutions not from the general wisdom of the society but from the rational analysis of individuals whose knowledge and morality are far beyond those of most people.

Confidence grants such individuals the right to frame solutions to social problems; confidence also demands that they actively seek to bring others up to the same level of knowledge, social sensitivity, and morality. And the confident expert can impose his solution on others if that is what their elevation requires. Compared to the power of the advanced individual, informed with facts and applying rational principles to solve problems, the collectively gained wisdom of the ages is so much organized superstition.

So a confident student goes to school not for selfish reasons but to "make a difference" in the world. By acquiring knowledge, the student also gains both the power and the duty to create social benefits for others—even if others are not yet advanced enough to appreciate those benefits. If the student chooses to become an oncologist, that expertise may well reflect general intellectual powers that can apply to trade policy or pedagogy as well.

Sowell argues effectively that cautious social policy is less concerned with equality and more concerned with the dangers of unequal power. The cautious vision sees "social responsibility" as outside the competence of businessmen. They may well predict their profits for the next quarter, but they have no special insight into the social benefits that may result, for example, from a particular hiring policy or a decision not to import from a politically odious country. The same is clearly true for others who may be knowledgeable about their own trade or profession, but cannot know whether practicing it will truly benefit society.

The social policy of the confident vision, however, is to seek greater equality in social conditions at the price of inequality in powers of decision-making—what Sowell calls the "locus of discretion." Confidence trusts the wisest and best individuals to act as surrogate decision-makers for the rest of us; caution, regarding no one as very wise or very good, prefers to leave decision-making scattered as widely as possible.

A key insight in Sowell's work is the distinction between process and result. The cautious vision, unsure of outcomes it cannot predict, prefers to establish a process—of teaching students, of selecting a head of state, of conducting business—and is prepared to live with the results of that process. The confident vision, however, wants particular results and will accept only the processes that produce those results.

If we apply Sowell's analysis to North American education, we see at once that many of its ills spring from the conflict of the cautious and confident visions. While many of my examples come from my own experience as a Canadian educator, I believe the conflict exists in the education systems of most nations.

The Cautious Vision of Education

If caution sees little range between the most knowledgeable and the most ignorant, that does not mean it disparages education. But it sees education as, at best, a means of sharing the collective experience and values built up over generations. It expects educated persons to demonstrate considerable mastery of their specialized subjects, and general familiarity with a canon of traditional knowledge. But it also expects them to emerge from their schooling with a strong sense of their own limitations.

Cautious education therefore prefers a relatively fixed curriculum taught in a standard manner. The curriculum has evolved slowly, over centuries, and reflects the collective choices of many generations. Therefore it is worthwhile to learn Latin and Greek, the better to appreciate the enduring values of Sophocles and Tacitus and to use them to illuminate one's own life. The manner of teaching may leave many children baffled, bored, and even beaten. But if at least some children flourish and maintain the traditional knowledge and values, that is a tradeoff worth making. Those children will contribute that knowledge to their generation's collective store.

Such an education teaches caution even in subtle ways. For centuries, European children studied the classics in the mournful knowledge that modern humanity was sadly inferior to the giants of ancient times. To grasp at least some of their wisdom was to escape barbarism. To prefer the modern authorities was to abandon enduring excellence for glib mediocrity. As late as the age of Jonathan Swift, the battle of ancients and moderns was still a lively one and the moderns did not seem fated to win.

Education in the cautious vision is a process; all enter

it on equal terms. While innate individual differences will ensure different results, the differences are not really great. Though one child may translate Virgil with ease, while another knows "little Latin and less Greek," caution sees both as still painfully limited by ignorance and selfishness. So the Virgil scholar has no particular qualification for taking charge of his slower classmate's life and making major decisions for him.

But the cautious vision has been on the defensive in education for some time, and often for good reason. It had served for centuries to train the ruling class and its middle managers in the clergy and professions. Advances in science and technology, especially since the Industrial Revolution, lent new credibility to the confident vision of man as problem-solver. Moreover, the new industries demanded ever-larger numbers of literate, numerate workers. Familiarity with Tacitus was no longer enough.

The confident vision has been in the ascendant for much of the last two centuries. The successes of science and technology have helped to foster the idea that knowledge of any kind endows its possessor with both power and morality. Confidence believes that new knowledge—gained through some form of the scientific method—is *ipso facto* superior to the folk wisdom that makes the cautious appear so backward. As new technology makes old technology obsolete, new learning throws old learning onto history's proverbial ash heap.

Confidence also breaks a crucial loyalty of the present to the past, making all social and personal commitments contingent on new information. Students once read the classics precisely because they were old and dealt with ingrained human concerns. Now their very age tells against them: they lack relevance in a world swamped by new, improved data and ideas. A book on computers published in 1985 is essentially useless; how then can a book published in 1885, or 1785, be worth anything?

For today's cautious parents, the success of the confident vision over the last century has created an ironic predicament. They clamor for traditional schools with traditional curriculum and teaching methods, and they often get them—whether by enrolling their children in private schools, or by forcing their local school boards to establish them within the public system. Such a back-to-basics public school recently opened in Surrey, B.C., with 200 students and an equal number on the waiting list. Doubtless hundreds of similar schools have sprung up in recent years.

Yet these traditional schools really reflect the values of the confident vision of the early 20th century—not of the true, classically oriented cautious education. In an attempt to keep more children in school longer, and to equip them with workplace skills rather than with cautious values, North America "watered down" the curriculum as early as the First World War. Cautious critics saw with horror the adoption of vocational programs catering to non-academic children who by rights should be learning work skills in the workplace, at their own expense and that of their employers. And far from teaching humility and caution, the academic schools of the early 20th century promoted a confident (if not arrogant) elitism. Their students went on to win two world wars, build nuclear weapons and spacecraft, and attempt to impose confident North American solutions to everyone else's problems.

Nevertheless, parents holding the cautious vision prefer the confident vision of yesterday over the confident vision of today. If nothing else, it gives them a sense of regained control over their children's schooling, a feeling that they are once more in the "locus of discretion" rather than mutely accepting the expertise of education professionals about what is best for their children. Such parents tend to think of education in particular metaphors—for example, the school as department store where customers pick and choose, or the school as Olympics where rigorous standards promote competition and high achievement for at least a few. A metaphor may make parents feel better, but it is no guarantee of genuine improvement in education.

The Confident Vision of Education

While the confident vision is ascendant in education, it is far from unquestioned. And its internal contradictions, to use a Marxian term, may force it into very new directions.

Confidence expects specific *results* from the schools and does not much care about the processes it uses to get them. Those results are high graduation rates that allow more students access to high-income jobs and thereby to greater political power. The confident vision wants a society of equals, "empowered" (in the current buzzword) with knowledge that will solve problems forever rather than compromise with tradeoffs.

Yet it sees a society of serious inequality. Though the confident vision has dominated the schools for a century, North America somehow remains ruled by white males, oppressing women and visible minorities. Knowledge and skills—and therefore power—are far from equally shared. Social problems abound, and problems must have solutions.

As Sowell points out, the confident vision believes that superior knowledge is both the means and the end of social improvement. A few advanced thinkers develop an understanding of a problem and a solution to it; their duty is then to act on behalf of the less advanced, creating conditions whereby others may also progress to a higher level of knowledge and morality.

Education is the obvious means to this end, and all the more so because it provides access to employment, higher income, and greater individual power to counter that of the present elite. If education appears to put some individ-

uals at a political or economic disadvantage, that is a failure
of the schools and the society that sets the schools'
agenda—not of the individuals.

In modern North America, therefore, the confident vision must seek 100 percent graduation rates and 100 percent employment—with all major social groups "represented"
proportionally in every occupation. If some students drop
out or fail, that is an unacceptable result and the system
must change its processes until the desired results appear.
Since new knowledge is superior to old, innovation is by
definition superior to traditional knowledge and should
produce superior results. If it does not, no matter; something still newer will be along soon.

The confident vision, like that of caution, must endure
its share of irony. If knowledge grants superior status and
higher responsibility, then educators—in the name of making society more equal and democratic—must control the
"locus of discretion" in the education of children. Parents,
employers, and the general public may think they know
what education should be, and what kind of society it
should serve. But educators alone really know what is best
for students and for society.

I hope I am not being unfair to my colleagues in saying
this. No doubt every profession feels it knows best about
its subject, and resents criticism from the outsiders it serves.
But the assumptions of the confident vision are now so
ingrained that educators rarely even trouble to examine
them. So educators feel baffled by the hostility of many
parents and the apparent apathy of the general public to
the problems in the schools. "If only they knew what we
know," teachers sigh. Criticism betrays the critics' ignorance, which automatically discredits their criticism.

But if special knowledge justifies special power, it also
encourages special pleading. A host of troubles follow. If
results are all that count, then any process which produces

high numbers of failures and dropouts is unacceptable. If necessary, educators will simply shrug, move the goal posts, and give C's to their F students. If anyone complains about grade inflation and declining standards, special pleading will argue that the old grading system was biased in favor of middle-class whites, or the old teaching method was culturally inappropriate, or the textbook failed to show positive role models of oppressed groups.

Perhaps that is true in some areas, but I have taught college English for almost thirty years in a predominantly white middle-class suburb that is among the best educated and most prosperous communities in Canada. Yet for me teaching "college English" has been largely what I see also being done in the primary grades: spelling, punctuation, grammar. However the schools may teach it, the result has been a large majority of graduates who are only nominally literate. As university graduates come into my classes in search of employable skills, I have learned that even a BA is no guarantee of basic literacy. Such students will not improve markedly in one or two semesters of college, but I cannot afford to flunk them all any more than my high-school and university colleagues can.

Under pressure from unhappy employers, my colleagues have now authorized me and my fellow English instructors to grade on a much harder scale. While this has led to some increase in failures, its chief effect has been grade deflation—bringing B students down to C or C–, and making A students much rarer. We instructors are much happier, but our students are furious. With a lower grade point average they have more trouble qualifying for loans and scholarships, and may not get into desirable programs.

But our students are an unhappy few. Most North American students enter post-secondary with good prospects even if they are utterly unprepared. Many are from ethnic groups or social classes with no tradition of respect

for academic study. They should fail; but failure is an unacceptable result and must be due to "systemic racism and
sexism" or some other lapse in process.

That is why grade inflation has moved into the post-
secondary system; why elaborate bureaucracies now look
after the affairs of disadvantaged students; why, if all else
fails, they can go into "studies" programs focussed on the
concerns of their particular group.

But before that happens, the confident educator is prepared to impose some very high process costs in the name
of future equality and justice. Students in "equity groups"
find they qualify for admission without the high test scores
demanded of others. If such students feel alienated by a
curriculum that rarely refers to them, they can dismiss it
as so much old junk by dead white European males, and
instead study recent work by members of their own group.
With luck they will never encounter an idea that challenges
their present values; if they do, they can reject it as "offensive." If it comes from their white professors they may
simply drive them off campus and perhaps end their careers, as happened not long ago at the University of Toronto.

The confident educator may well recognize the flaws in
this policy. "Yes," he will say, "racism is the treatment of
people based on what they are and not what they do, and
we do treat people differently depending on what they are.
Yes, we demand less of some students than we do of others,
and less of everyone than we once did. Yes, we reject our
old curriculum—and our own education—because the
canon doesn't succeed with these new students. But this
process cost is a price worth paying because it will lead to
greater equality."

The price is higher still. Confident educators themselves
must be equals, and every school should reflect the sexual
and ethnic diversity of the community it serves. Hence the
growth of employment equity, with preferential hiring of

persons who can claim affinity with some oppressed or dis-advantaged group—whether they themselves have suffered or not.

This issue has arisen on my own campus, and it alarms me as much as anything has in over a quarter-century of teaching. I take some pride in my involvement in the U.S. civil-rights movement in the 1960s, and in having written a history of British Columbia's black pioneers in the 1970s. The idea that I should now judge potential faculty on the basis of their race and sex, and hire accordingly, seems like the revenge of a cruel but witty God. The confident vision, having fought racism and sexism in the name of equality, is now willing to entrench those vicious practices as a mere process cost, and to build yet more luxurious ghettoes for those whom it promised to liberate.

Confidence has also cast a chill on academic freedom; whatever seems to question the confident vision is a threat to equality, freedom, justice, and empowerment. Academics must revise their reading lists, not only to include newly favored authorities but also to remove those with danger-ous views and embarrassing language. Classroom discussion must avoid inappropriate opinions or someone will launch a suit for harassment.

A cynical believer in the cautious vision would say it doesn't matter because education has long since ceased to be the purpose of the schools: it simply serves as a kind of welfare system for educated unemployables, who can ar-range their affairs any way they like because they are not really doing anything useful.

"Of course the kids are packing weapons to school," the cynic would say. "If you expelled every kid who carried a gun or knife, your graduation rates would look even worse than they do. Of course they're illiterate; if you held them back instead of promoting them, they'd drop out in even greater numbers. Of course they're getting pregnant at fourteen; they can still go to school and the school will look after their babies. Of course you're hiring on the basis of race, sex and disability; once competence no longer matters, everyone deserves a proportional share of the pie."

The cynic might also rudely note that the confident vision predicts that desirable social results will spring from particular teaching practices; yet generations of confident education have not yet produced the egalitarian Utopia that is supposed to justify all the process costs like school lunches, affirmative-action hiring, and grade inflation.

The Stereoscopic Vision

The cautious vision, for all the wisdom it has accumulated over the centuries, has much foolishness to apologize for. In its caution it has squandered the intellectual, cultural, and economic potential of individuals and groups who might have enriched everyone, because they were not recognized, authorized sources of orthodox wisdom. For its masters it has provided convenient endorsement of brutally expedient policies, and as a "vision" it is dangerously myopic.

In its concern with process over results, caution is too often satisfied with clumsy processes that guarantee poor results; then it stupidly defines those results as excellence because they succeed so rarely. Sowell observes that few businessmen are advocates for the cautious or constrained vision. No wonder: a business as inefficient as most cautious processes would soon go broke. The tradeoff that caution settles for is all too often simply a ripoff, a transfer of costs elsewhere: onto a worker, a student, a consumer, a citizen—or onto the whole society and its environment.

If caution is myopic, confidence is too farsighted to see what's under its nose. Spellbound by a Utopia close enough to touch but too distant to grasp, it betrays its faith in knowledge by catering to ignorance; in the name of equality it imposes an oligarchy of educated, expert "progressives" ruling like colonialists over the less enlightened.

Unable to run an effective faculty meeting, those with the confident vision still think they ought to run the world. Some, who have had a smattering of a cautious education, may be able to quote Cicero: *Nihil tam absurde dici potest, quod non dicatur ab aliquo philosophorum*—Nothing is so absurd but some philosopher has said it. But they would not apply such an observation to themselves.

While the foolish intellectual has been a figure of fun since Aristophanes put Socrates in Cloud-Cuckoo-Land, the confident vision has led some intellectuals to become dreadful scourges of their societies: Pol Pot of the Khmer Rouge had a good French education, and Abimael Guzman, the leader of the Sendero Luminoso, was a philosophy professor before he went into the mountains. Confidence has quite as much to apologize for as caution does.

Damage to a particular part of the brain can not only cause blindness in one eye, but can destroy the victim's entire perception of that side: the left or right simply does not exist any more, whether in one's own body, on a page, or in the world. In the country of the blind the one-eyed man may be king; in the country of the one-eyed, of the single vision, the king must have two eyes or he will lead his people nowhere.

Caution and confidence arise in opposition to one another, and each needs the other. Caution keeps confidence from launching itself into folly. Confidence prods caution out of its dull complacency and makes it think. Unchallenged, either vision will become a pathologically distorted view of the world.

Thomas Sowell is right when he says truth may not always lie conveniently between the two visions: "It may. It may not. On some highly specific issue, it may lie entirely on one side—and on another issue, with the other side. On still other issues, it may in fact lie in between." What he does not say, however, is that it often lies on both sides.

We will not be able to find the truth if our commitment to one vision is so total that we automatically dismiss the evidence the other vision offers. In education especially, we need both visions if we are going to see the real world in three dimensions.

Like many others of my generation, I became an educator in part out of the confident belief that I could help raise others to a higher level of thought, understanding, and social involvement. Before long I had learned caution: much that was new was useless as curriculum and method, and much that was old was almost magically effective. My students' cautious conventionality made me despair for the future; yet they taught me to respect them as sensibly cautious fellow-citizens even as I tried to prod them into thinking confident new thoughts.

When I taught in China in 1983, I saw that my students and teaching colleagues were living paradoxes. Chinese communism, though founded on the confident vision, had ruled so long that it had become a cautious tyranny; it even persecuted dissidents for "thinking they know better than the Party," a sin against caution and collective wisdom if ever I heard one.

My students, the Communist Party's privileged sons and daughters, had nevertheless become independent thinkers—and I found myself far more cautious than they. Though I could have put Orwell's *Nineteen Eighty-Four* on my reading list, I decided it was too dangerous; it might get my students in trouble by making them think they knew better than the Party.

Then I found that my Chinese colleagues were teaching Orwell's "Politics and the English Language." While Orwell was a socialist exponent of the confident vision, his essay is one of the greatest modern condemnations of the smelly little orthodoxies that have arisen from both visions. The students took Orwell to heart, dismissed the orthodoxies, and pursued their personal interests like disciples of Adam Smith. In fact, the school's top student, the son of a major Party official in Swatow, now works for an advertising agency in Chicago. So much for the Communist Party's half-century of confident planning and cautious collective wisdom.

I came home from China no longer able to think in terms of right or left, progressive or reactionary, and the world has looked different to me ever since. My confident colleagues have developed an almost Chinese caution: after all, confidence has been the received wisdom of the last several generations and it wouldn't do to criticize that wisdom. Those holding the cautious vision, meanwhile—whether doctrinaire Friedmanites in the Fraser Institute or fundamentalist Christians spurning secular values—are alarmingly confident that their views will benefit the larger society as well as themselves.

To return to Thomas Sowell's terms, my vision alternates between the constrained and the unconstrained, between a stoic acceptance of the real and a romantic hunger for something better. When the visions conflict the world seems blurred and hallucinatory; but when they blend, they show me a world that offers both joy in the present and hope for the future. In what follows, I hope I can keep those visions blended.

2

Rethinking School

The Lesson of Little Fort

A few one-room schools still survive in western Canada, though probably not for much longer. Most people think of them as relics of a primitive era when semiliterate farmers grudgingly provided the least possible education for their children. But one such school in British Columbia would be a good place to start if we want to rethink our ideas about school.

Little Fort, ninety-three kilometers north of Kamloops, B.C., is a farming community in the North Thompson River country. Settled in the 1890s, it's had a one-room school since 1908. The original building burned down in the mid-1930s. Its replacement, when I visited it in 1990, held twenty students, teacher Cathy Shave, and her aide Maureen Brown. Administratively it was an annex of Barriere Ridge School, thirty minutes' drive south down the Yellowhead Highway.

Little Fort School's pupils ranged from five-year-old kindergartners to ten-year-olds in Grade 5. One child was an aspiring writer; another had special needs and required the aide's attention. In effect, the pupils needed six different curriculums. Most teachers would shrink from such a job. Teaching a split class with just two age levels is considered tough enough. Cathy Shave disagreed.

"It's an incredibly wonderful experience to teach in a one-room school," she said.

When she and her husband Ed Nagy decided to move to the country and she learned about Little Fort, she applied specifically for the school. She was lucky it still existed. In the mid-80s its population had fallen to just eight children and it seemed likely to close. With newcomers moving into the region, however, Little Fort School won a reprieve.

She admitted the first year was somewhat daunting. It was a far cry from her previous experience—four years in Summerland, B.C., and nine in suburban North Vancouver. Here she was on her own; her nearest colleagues were half an hour away in Barriere. If anything went wrong, she would have no one to fall back on. In bigger schools, she added, "Discipline problems require colleague support. Here, they're just not an issue."

Classes certainly weren't like a regular school's. The day began at 8:30 with everyone in the story corner for a singsong and conversation. Cathy played guitar while the kids belted out "Feelin' Groovy" and "Rock My Soul in the Bosom of Abraham." Then she assigned children to their tasks: the kindergartners swarmed to their table, while the older students scattered to the other three or four small tables in the classroom. The mood was both relaxed and industrious. When the teacher had shown the kindergartners what she wanted them to do, she checked on the older ones. No one minded if a kindergartner came over to share a table.

"With multigrades and a small number of kids," said Cathy, "the children become more a family than a class. They're all the same peer group, all friends."

The effect in the classroom was startling. Older children accepted younger ones cheerfully and matter-of-factly. No

one tried to monopolize the teacher's or the class's atten-
tion. During recess and lunch, everyone played together.
Supervision was not a major concern. "The big ones look
after the little ones," Cathy said. "They're very sensible.
They know that if anyone gets hurt, it's half an hour to
Barriere or half an hour to Clearwater to get help."

The school's facilities were sparse but adequate. An extra
room held everything from a piano to a hand-me-down
Commodore 64 computer and a small kitchen. The basement served as a gym. The classroom itself was bright and
airy, with room for tables, bookshelves, "wiggle and jiggle"
space, and a treasured photocopier.

Instead of trying to tailor a separate curriculum to each
age group, Little Fort School used themes: whales, Canada,
bats, even bubbles. Children worked at their own level
within the theme. Some of their work appeared in a com-
puter-produced school newsletter.

"It's quite a balancing act," Cathy told me. "You adjust
your expectations to the grade level."

When they move to a bigger school in Barriere for
Grade 6, Little Fort kids are "shining lights," principal
Gilles Joubert told me later. "They've learned to become
independent workers; they adapt quite well."

Supposedly a relic of the past, Little Fort was really a
vision of a very attractive future. It didn't make me feel
nostalgic for some idealized little red schoolhouse—just
frustrated that most children spend twelve years in a big
beige factory. I looked forward to a whole province full of
Little Forts.

In the early 1990s, however, the recession frightened
educators and politicians into a kind of emotional regres-
sion: they deserted the confident vision of the Year 2000
program and began to clamor for "standards" that would
make children "competitive" in the "global economy." Instead of dealing with each child as an individual, these new
fundamentalists see children as counters in some planetary

game of Risk. What the children want or need is beside the point; their only function is to be a kind of infantry in the trenches of a global economic war.

Well, let us think again about the preconceptions and misconceptions we have acquired about education and its purpose in the North America of the late 20th century.

"Now, When I Was Going To School . . ."

Every time you pick up a paper or magazine, someone is telling you how really awful today's education is. Magazines warn parents to "school-proof" their children against the mess in our classrooms. Books protest the "catastrophe" in the schools. Columnists sigh nostalgically about strict old Miss Strapwell back in the '40s or '50s. Boy, she really knew how to teach the basics.

By contrast, they tell us, today's teachers—addle-brained relics of the '60s—hate competition, fret over any threat to children's delicate self-esteem, and spend their numerous professional-development days learning how to ignore parents. Meanwhile Chinese and Japanese students (always in classes of at least fifty) are achieving astronomical test scores and leaving our kids in their dust. We can't compete because our teachers can't teach and our students can't learn.

Sorry, I've heard it all before. Almost forty years ago. When the Soviets launched Sputnik in 1957, North America's media enjoyed a good cry about our lousy schools. In 1958 *Life* magazine ran a cover story comparing a grinning airhead American teenager and a serious, studious young Russian. Academically, Alexei was two years ahead of fun-loving Stephen.

The magazine's attack on the previous quarter-century of miseducation (that is, all the way back to 1933) could have been written this week: "shockingly low" standards, overcrowding, too many elective courses, no agreement about what schools should teach. Critics moaned about devalued diplomas, stupid teachers, lazy students, and lax parents.

According to the 1950s media, dear old Miss Strapwell had screwed up. Far from demanding excellence, she had coddled her students into a coma. The Russians had beaten the west into orbit because they had beaten us in the classroom. Canadian studies, like Hilda Neatby's *So Little for the Mind* in 1953 and the 1960 Chant Commission on B.C. schools, confirmed the American verdict. So floods of money poured into the schools. Even as the post-secondary system expanded, college applicants faced cut-throat competition for the available seats. Students lived or died by their standardized test scores.

Since I was part of the airhead generation, my own education was deeply suspect even though I had spent eighteen months at a British-run private school in Mexico City and another couple of years at the American School—a walled enclave of Yankee elitism in the middle of a foul slum. Whatever advantage I had gained in learning a little Latin soon dissipated when I entered high school in Santa Monica, California—a heaven for surfers, but no Parnassus on the Pacific.

Somehow, despite my media-confirmed inadequacies, I got into Columbia University, where our professors made no effort to conceal their contempt for us. They despised us as a conformist "silent generation" of illiterates ruined by TV, comic books, and lax standards. If you listened to the professors, politicians, and columnists of the late 1950s, you knew that rigorously schooled Russian communists would make short work of dopes like us.

Well, it was the Russians who ended up in history's ashcan. The students of the '60s can take a lot of the credit. As scientists, engineers, business people, academics, authors, artists, and musicians, we largely created today's world. No doubt we deserve our share of blame for what's gone wrong (and plenty has). As Calvin Trillin once observed, middle age is depressing because you realize the jerks you went to school with are now running everything. But we jerks run a world that escaped nuclear war and is struggling away from totalitarianism.

A fat lot of thanks we get. Teachers of the '60s generation are supposed to be so fuzzy-minded and slack that their students can't compete with the Chinese and Japanese. The critics haven't noticed that China and Japan import *our* teachers, not the other way around. And the best of Asia's students head for North American campuses every chance they get; they find workloads and standards a lot higher than back home.

So don't believe all the laments. One of the consolations of middle age is to flatter your own education by criticizing that of your kids. It's a very dangerous consolation, however, because it lets you avoid really thinking about why school was the way it was forty years ago, and how it might change in the next forty.

Blaming the Schools
One major cause of school criticism is economic anxiety. The early 1980s gave us food banks and teacher-bashing as a martial art. Governments called for education reform, moaned about the threat of Japanese competition, and generally despaired about our economic prospects.

The moaning stopped, briefly, during the Gulf War. Somehow the inadequate schools of North America had managed to produce both sophisticated weapons and highly effective soldiers trained to use them. (That the war happened at all, however, did not speak well for the education of George Bush and his allies like Brian Mulroney.) Now our economy is back on life support and once again politicians and business executives lament the decline of standards in education.

The same thing happened in 1932 during the Depression. Plenty of British Columbians felt schools had gone to the dogs. Many complained that standards had collapsed because of airy-fairy progressive education. Schools, critics charged, were fooling around with a child-centered curriculum. Innovations like junior high schools were a waste of money. So was that newfangled vocational education, which was just a gimmick to keep kids in school even if they couldn't handle real subjects like Latin.

The provincial Tory government of the day appointed Vancouver businessman George Kidd to study government spending; his report took special aim at education. Kidd wanted teachers to pay the whole cost of their own training, and he also wanted to cut teacher salaries by twenty-five percent. Students between fourteen and sixteen should pay half the cost of their schooling, and anyone still in school over age sixteen should pay 100 percent. As for post-secondary, Kidd proposed shutting down the University of British Columbia altogether. Deserving students might get scholarships to universities "elsewhere in the Dominion."

No one would accept the Kidd Report today. But we still pretend our economic health will return if only we bring back the education system that got us into this mess in the first place.

Much criticism of education is the predictable result of pure future shock. This is not the world we expected, and it's natural to want to return to the known world of yesterday. The end of the Cold War showed that the West was prepared for everything except success; we were really quite comfortable living under the threat of annihilation, and many of us would gladly go back to it rather than deal with the present global anarchy.

Education reform, likewise, is ready to fight in the trenches forever, but not to consider the perils of victory. If we're serious about making schools better, we should realize we are asking for a radical political and social revolution. After all, if Native Indians stayed in school, they'd end up as scientists, engineers, doctors, and lawyers. Working-class kids would qualify for management jobs. Women and immigrants would push into even more fields than they now do. Society would change with terrifying speed, and it would never slow down. How could it, with everyone learning all the time? The confident vision wants this outcome but wouldn't know what to do if it achieved such a revolution.

The cautious vision, by contrast, doesn't believe for a moment that such a result is possible, but doesn't want to think about the social hazards of prolonging the status quo; it virtually guarantees change by refusing to consider it. This cautious attitude can bring out the worst in the confident vision, which decides in frustration that only extreme measures will work against cautious inertia. That happens in cautious countries that educate only a tiny elite. Think of Russia, China, Vietnam, and Cambodia—all brutalized and impoverished by their scholars. And their scholars were the product of elitist, "high standards" education that literally saw knowledge as power and legitimized any outrage as a process cost of maximizing equality. I'd rather take my chances with the first kind of revolution.

Defining Some Terms

Some of the most devastating criticism of education comes unintentionally from educators themselves, most of whom are incapable of expressing a clear, jargon-free sentence. Our profession is also as fond as teenagers of in-group slang, except that our slang lacks energy and resonance. To clear away the bafflegab, let's redefine some of the terms in the debate, while junking others altogether. But first we should realize that some crucial words have sharply different meanings for people holding conflicting visions.

In the cautious vision, "freedom" takes the preposition "from": freedom from outside interference leaves individuals at liberty to do as they please within their particular circumstances. An illiterate child and a millionaire, therefore, can both be free as long as no one else imposes on them. The confident vision dismisses this as utterly inadequate; its only freedom is one preceding an infinitive verb. Freedom to act is crucial, and any social conditions that preclude action are problems demanding solutions. So education is the prerequisite to freedom.

"Power" is another word with contrasting definitions. Thomas Sowell sees the confident defining the word as a result—"the possibility of imposing one's will on others." The cautious, however, define it as process: "restricting the choices of others."

Caution defines "equality" as a process also, which everyone undergoes but which has varying results. Confidence defines "equality" as a single result which may require varying processes to achieve.

So the first term on my hit list is the verb "empower." This is popular with confident educators because it hints at students (and other theoretically oppressed groups) imposing their will on other people for a change. It's sure to infuriate believers in the cautious vision, of course, since they see such empowerment as restricting their choices.

Let's drop "excellence" while we're at it. It's become a bureaucrat's buzzword; most educators would settle for plain competence in the schools. It can annoy believers in the confident vision, since it implies the superiority of some over others. For many cautious parents and educators, it's just a devastatingly ironic term for anything that isn't outright mediocre.

Next to go is "self-esteem." Educators still don't realize how the term makes cautious parents go crazy. Critics think it means touchy-feely flattery and puffing up kids' egos at the expense of all academic standards; sometimes they're right. After all, confident educators are pushing hard for equality and adopting whatever process will get that result. So forget self-esteem and call it self-respect or even self-definition. Students who expect a lot from themselves work harder than those who don't. Students who define themselves as good at math do better than those who define themselves as hopeless at math.

A negative self-definition is very hard to change. I see that with students who define themselves as bad spellers or slow learners when they're nothing of the sort. They often resist evidence of their own ability because it means confronting a whole new identity (and a lot more work). But when a positive self-definition does sink in, the student becomes unstoppable.

We should also consider three words that really need redefinition. Critics are always groaning about the "failure of education," without explaining what they mean. Education is actually a catch-all term for several distinct kinds of learning.

So I define *training* as "know how." Reading, for example, is a skill that requires training. You learn the arbitrary meanings of letters and the ways they combine into words, and the decoding process eventually becomes as automatic as knowing when to shift gears or how to swing a baseball bat. You might even say that training enables you to put something out of your mind and still do it.

Schooling is "know that." If students are ignorant even though they can read, that's a failure of schooling. The uproar over "cultural literacy" springs from anxiety over the fact that today's students have a different kind of schooling which leaves them ignorant of some facts that their elders consider vital.

Education is "know why." A student can know *how* to read, and thereby know *that* Shakespeare wrote *Hamlet*. But only an educated student knows why Shakespeare matters—and why reading itself is important. In other words, education is the instilling of an *attitude* toward learning— not learning itself. If the culture of the school fails to instill that attitude, then we do indeed have a failure of education.

So phonics versus whole language, for example, is an

issue in *training*. Ignorance of geography or history or math is an issue in *schooling*. People who graduate but never open another book—because they don't see a need to—are the real failures of *education*.

Obviously training, schooling and education are all essential. Students need to possess dozens of "hard skills," from reading to listening to keyboarding. They need to learn a large body of relevant information, or their skills become trivial. And they need an educated attitude toward learning, or the whole process will stop dead ten seconds after they finish their last exam. Self-respect based on competence is vital to that attitude.

Let me suggest another term that might clarify some issues and suggest the scale of the problems we face. When schools try to create a pro-education culture based on the confident vision, they are teaching swimming in the Sahara.

They try to teach the value of learning for its own sake, as well as the value of being a responsible citizen. But they have to fight the "anti-culture." This is an attitude that dominates society outside school—a contempt for intelligence, imagination, and social responsibility which springs ultimately from the cautious vision. Caution, after all, doesn't think highly of any individual's knowledge outside a narrow range of expertise.

In the anti-culture, the value of a book lies in the money it makes for its author. That's why stupid and trivial bestsellers are the only books that get much attention. The value of a musical composition lies in the money it makes for its composer and performers. Great paintings are of interest only because Japanese companies pay millions to own them. Grown men playing boys' games earn equal millions for a few afternoons' work on a basketball court or baseball field.

The worst thing that the anti-culture can say about crime is that it doesn't pay. Therefore anything that doesn't pay is a kind of crime. And anything that *does* pay isn't really a crime at all—including the presentation of criminal violence, cruelty, and abuse as children's entertainment.

The anti-culture teaches its own values to everyone it can reach. Most newspapers and magazines are textbooks in the anti-culture curriculum. Almost every TV show, radio program and movie is an audiovisual aid promoting anti-culture values. And what are those values? The world-shaking importance of the sex lives and income of athletes and entertainers. The financial success of big dumb movies. The financial success of loud dumb songs. Violence as the solution to every problem. Shopping as the purpose of life.

Apart from sentimental appeals at Christmas time, the anti-culture feels absolutely no responsibility for anyone except immediate family and friends—maybe not even them. So the anti-culture of the cautious vision has caused the decay of civic values and civility itself. It glorifies private prosperity amid public squalor. It feels apathy for the homeless and unemployed, hatred for public servants and public institutions, contempt for democracy itself. Hypocritically, the anti-culture then gets hysterical about the violence, racism, ignorance, and general misery that it's encouraged.

This is why the schools stagger from crisis to crisis. People who believe in the anti-culture of the cautious vision obviously don't give a damn about an education system largely dominated by the confident vision.

Thoroughly trained in the anti-culture by the age of five, children come into our classrooms already biased against the love of learning, critical thinking, and knowledge itself. We appear to them as invaders, an occupying force trying to impose alien values on them. At every opportunity they repudiate what we teach and uphold the anti-culture.

Educators struggle with the conflict between the culture of the confident vision and the anti-culture variety of the cautious vision. We know that young people want, need, and deserve an economic role as they grow into adults. But we also know that the real purpose of making money is to do things that don't make money. People make money so they can afford to go skiing, grow flowers, listen to music, travel, write unpublishable novels, raise their kids.

If we educators really believe in what we're doing, it's time to go on the attack against the anti-culture. Until we do, we'll keep trying to swim through sand.

Some of what follows may itself sound like anti-culture propaganda, because eventually I am going to propose a sharp reduction in the length, scope, and uniformity of publicly funded education at all levels. Before that, however, I want to suggest ways the education bureaucracy can make itself more efficient and responsive—the "restructuring" that most people think is all we need. Every system has the right to defend itself, and the schools certainly have that right.

But restructuring is at best a holding action, a fighting retreat to protect the children and teachers still in the system. No matter how efficient and responsive it can make itself, the education bureaucracy will become a begged question within the next ten or fifteen years. If people who care about education can break out of their habits of thought, they can shorten the period of turbulence before a new system stabilizes, and thereby ensure a better education for the children of the 21st century. If they cling to their old habits, the turbulence will persist just as it has for the last couple of decades. It will be noisy, exciting, but aimless—in effect, a kind of dynamic stagnation.

And the Purpose of Education?
What is education for, anyway?

The present debate has largely ignored that basic question. Instead, critics have attacked the schools for not calming our economic anxieties. Every few weeks, yet another politician or economist or corporation executive discovers that we have a lot of dropouts and relatively poor scores on international achievement tests. These shocking findings inspire public lamentation about our lack of "competitiveness."

But, how, exactly, are we supposed to compete? If we teach more math and physics, will Canada be able to sell VCRS to Japan and luxury cars to Germany? If we send more people to college, will we outproduce the Mexicans working in *maquiladora* factories?

The unspoken premise of the competitiveness argument is that students are simply pawns in someone else's economic game. The game's purpose is to create enough wealth so you (or your rulers) can push other people around while avoiding being pushed yourself. To play this game we need economic growth, whatever the cost to our environment and society. To maintain a growing economy based on resource extraction and manufacturing, we need a well-educated population. They need not only the right skills but the right attitudes. They have to believe that wealth equals consumption and consumption equals happiness. We don't ask our children if they want to play this game, and we certainly don't teach them to question it. We just scream at them (and their teachers) if they don't learn the rules.

On one level I accept the competitiveness argument. We've all seen some of our trading partners push us around because we're economically too weak to push back. I've done my share of moaning about the economic harm we do ourselves by failing to educate all our children. And most of my teaching has been to equip students with job skills. But the 55-billion-dollar enterprise called Canadian education is not just a huge subsidy to our corporate employers and political masters. Its real purpose ought to be the training of free men and women.

But what do we mean by freedom? For the cautious vision, freedom is "freedom from"—from government

intervention, from social pressure. In the cautious definition, free people make their own choices and have plenty
to choose from. For the confident vision, however, freedom
is "freedom to"—to act, to speak, to exercise power. Simply
to leave people alone without the power to act is to abandon them to oppression. People who know calculus are
free to seek a wider range of careers than those who don't.
People who have more income are free to spend more of
it as they please. The real horror of an ill-educated population is lack of freedom however we define it, not lack of
economically useful skills. If we are badly schooled, others
will indeed push us around—everyone from our own welfare bureaucrats to Japanese bankers and American manu-
facturers.

This is the message we have failed to get across to our
children. We have shown zero interest in making them
free enough to choose their own destiny; we reward them
only when they go along with the game plan. We've told
them that their purpose in life is to be economic cannon
fodder—assets to entice investors into building new saw-
mills or software companies. So we shouldn't be surprised
if many of them reject school and all it stands for.

Free citizens know they also have responsibilities, and
that they must indeed learn well if they are to work well,
prosper, and thereby protect their freedom. When our children see that we really do want to make them free—all of
them—then they will learn very well indeed.

Another useful way to look at our preconceptions is with
what teachers call the Data to Wisdom chain. It has a couple of versions, but the one I like best goes like this:

Data organized is information.
Information made meaningful is knowledge.
Knowledge applied to other knowledge is intelligence.
Intelligence granted experience is wisdom.

Simple enough, even self-evident, but these linked definitions have alarming implications—not just for educators

but for everyone. For example, if intelligence is knowledge applied to other knowledge, then stupidity is the failure to connect the things we already know. If our grandparents smoked, they were ignorant. If we smoke, knowing what we do about the health dangers of tobacco, we're just stupid.

Teachers can see their link in the chain. Scientists and other scholars dig up the data and organize it into information. Our job is to make it meaningful knowledge to our students. The better we teach, the more they learn. But it follows, however, that great stupidity depends on great knowledge. Only the highly educated, by definition, are capable of it. And here the chain tightens around us.

Education critics (all of whom are highly educated) clamor about the need to make our students "competitive" with their counterparts in the U.S., Europe, and especially Asia. But competitive at what? Solving quadratic equations? Memorizing the dates of England's kings? No one gives a damn about abstract knowledge. Captains of industry and political leaders want our kids to be able to slug it out economically with foreign kids.

In other words, the critics of education want Canadian students to be extremely skilled at ripping the last penny of wealth out of our forests and fields and mines. They don't want the Japanese to clearcut Malaysia and the Philippines before we've clearcut B.C. They don't want Canadians to have to take the bus because they're too poor to own smog-belching cars.

They do, however, want Canadians to consume as much as possible of the world's energy and resources, regardless of consequences that we can clearly foresee. In effect, they want Canadians to be stupid on a scale never before imagined.

From the Mayans to the Mesopotamians, advanced civilizations have used their learning only to destroy themselves by destroying their resources. Educators know this, yet we seem unable to teach that lesson to our students. After all, if we did, we'd be telling them that their parents (who pay our salaries by ripping out Canada's resources) are stupid. And no one has seriously suggested since the 1960s that teaching really should be a subversive activity.

The Mayans and Mesopotamians were ignorant; we are stupid. If we are really serious about building a sustainable society, we will have to stop teaching the philosophy of endless growth. We'll have to show our students that our gaudy civilization of shopping malls and freeways has no more right to live than a cancer does.

To do that, however, educators will also have to persuade this nation that we must teach our children to repudiate their parents' whole lifestyle. Does that seem stupid to you? Then correlate your knowledge and try to find a more intelligent conclusion that will stand the test of experience long enough to become wisdom.

Unaffordable Luxuries

The bureaucratic, confident-vision school model has some wonderful, but very expensive, philosophical premises. I think we will have to abandon or heavily revise them, but first we should examine them again.

- *Everyone is entitled to an education.* No argument.
- *All citizens are politically equal, regardless of race, sex, class or ethnicity.* No argument.
- *Everyone is entitled to an equal education.* Now we're in trouble. The education of a Westmount teenager is simply not going to be "equal" to that of a Lillooet teenager, no matter how we define equality. A seriously disabled child is not going to get an education equal to a fully able one, no matter how much time they spend together in the same classroom. An emotionally disturbed child from an abusive background can never get the education of a happy, nurtured child. We recognize that, but we don't like it; accepting it

feels like accepting entrenched privilege and systemic bias. So we adopt another premise:

- *Where disparities exist, the schools' obigation is to erase them.* In some cases this is both self-evident and easy; in others, it is neither. We can provide equivalent facilities, learning materials, and rewards for students.

But we confident educators have a bad habit: When we recognize a problem like dropouts, physical disability or learning disorders, we hire some knowledgeable expert (usually without the problem) to address it. Such services are admirable. But they cost money that could serve the schools and students more directly, and they never eliminate themselves. No matter how well we address the problems, they all require people on the payroll, locking the schools into ever-growing contributions to benefits packages, unemployment insurance, and so on. We then need to hire even more people to look after the increased paperwork.

A more advanced future civilization will regard with distaste a society in which many of the educated middle classes owed their incomes, jobs, and prestige to the social misery of their clients. Our descendants will not think much, either, of our readiness to identify our own middle class well-being as school employees with the well-being of education itself.

- *The ideal teaching environment is a classroom with not too many students, all of whom should be about the same age.* The ideal teaching environment in most cases is a pupil-teacher ratio of 1:1. We group children in classes because we can't afford individual tutors except in special cases. Grouping by age is administratively convenient; otherwise it's not very useful. Children learn extremely well from other children of different ages (especially their siblings), though parents and teachers don't always approve of *what* they learn.
- *The present school system is permanent.* We may talk of

reform and restructuring, but not of replacement. That is because hundreds of thousands of educators— and their fellow citizens—depend on it for a living just as the Sioux depended on the buffalo and Maritimers depended on the northern cod.

In many Canadian communities, the local school district, community college or university is the largest single employer and one of the largest single customers for carpenters, electricians, plumbers, painters, stationers, gardeners, cooks, auto mechanics, and other tradespersons. All depend on education business. Their needs inevitably take precedence over those of children. After all, adults vote; children don't.

Much of the present conflict about education stems from our efforts to change the system without really changing these premises. Those efforts are futile.

3

The Demographic Avalanche

Anecdotal Evidence

When I was a small boy growing up in Mexico in the early 1950s, I was a voracious reader of science fiction and fantasy. This was still the age of the American pulp magazines, and they were readily available even in Mexico City, which was then a sleepy village of only three million. My parents worried about my literary taste or lack thereof, and sometimes tried to discourage my consumption of science fiction and fantasy.

I'm sure they meant well. They wanted to prepare me for the real world, but they couldn't foresee the future. How could they know that by dosing myself with pulp science fiction and fantasy, I was receiving ideal preparation for a career as a British Columbia school trustee and teacher?

My formal education at that point revolved around a private school run by expatriate Britons. For all their radical, confident-vision politics, my parents thought that such an education would suit me and my brother very well. So, while George Bernard Shaw and George VI died, and a young Princess Elizabeth ascended to the throne, I learned rudimentary Latin, British history, and how to convert pounds and shillings into pence and halfpence. All this in a Spanish-speaking nation that didn't even yet know it was part of the Third World.

I look back on it now with some fondness, for all that it was a sublimely irrelevant education for the world I now live in. But I do recognize that it tried to draw me into a cultural, social, and political matrix that had flourished around the world for a century or more. Mackenzie King, Jawaharlal Nehru, and Jomo Kenyatta would have recognized my curriculum.

Much of the schools' task boils down to maintaining such a matrix, and using it to keep a continuity with the past while adapting to an increasing pace of change. That job gets harder every year, and we educators—whether we hold the confident or the cautious vision—feel increasingly threatened by the changes that sweep the past away. Not only does it make our own past seem inconsequential, but we know that barbarism is the state of ignorance of one's own history. That's why we sometimes look at our students and shudder; they haven't even *heard* of Mackenzie King, Jawaharlal Nehru, or Jomo Kenyatta.

I suspect we all look back at our own schooling with some nostalgia, while worrying about what kind of future we're creating for our children. We may even be tempted to forget about the future because it looks too grim.

Order versus Chaos

As a science-fiction writer, I *can't* forget about the future. It's where I make a good part of my income, and where I expect to spend the rest of my life. I want to discuss our future as Canadians—people who may have a decisive effect on the life of this country well into the next century. If we're conscious of our influence as educators, parents, and citizens, the confident vision promises we can educate for everyone's good; if we prefer the cautious vision, we're likely to be battered by events. I want to argue that we can best serve the interests of our students and our society by creating schools for chaos.

You might think that "schools for chaos" are the direct opposite of what we're supposed to be doing in the classroom. Chaos is what breaks out when the teacher leaves the room or fails to maintain order. It's an open challenge to everything we teachers are dedicated to, and if we can't restore order we feel we've gone into the wrong profession.

We educators believe in order and predictability. So do our bureaucratic and political masters. Everyone is confident that if we teachers do our jobs right, our students will leave our classrooms with predictable knowledge—how to do quadratic equations, the name of Canada's first prime minister, the location of Australia on a map. They'll need this knowledge, we say confidently, to cope with the real world in the future. The politicians and bureaucrats are equally confident that we can supply them with predictably well-trained workers for the economy of the 21st century, though they don't say how they can foresee its needs.

We are all probably wrong.

Belief in a predictable, clockwork universe goes back to Isaac Newton, who showed that mathematics can forecast much of the future. But many scientists are growing doubtful about clockwork predictability. They are finding that chaos rules the systems they study.

Chaos doesn't mean turbulence and confusion and kids screaming in the classroom. It means *built-in unpredictability*. In effect, when a system becomes complicated enough, *no one* can tell what it will do next. Society in this sense is chaotic, just like the weather. So many factors are at work that we simply can't tell what some given factor will do in conjunction with millions of other factors.

Educators are in the business of making society even more complicated. The more that people know, the more skills they possess, the harder it is to predict their future behavior. Sure, in the short run we can predict that most students, after studying Chapter 6 in their textbooks, will be able to do quadratic equations. But will they still know how in two months? In twenty years? And if so, for what purpose?

The parents and educators of the 1950s and '60s must have had some future in mind when they decided how to educate today's adults. But let's imagine that we can rent Michael J. Fox's time-travelling DeLorean and drive into Vancouver or Toronto for a meeting of local school trustees and teachers in, say, 1960. They're waiting to hear what the 1980s and '90s will really be like, so they can design the appropriate school system and curriculum.

Suppose we tell them to prepare their children to face environmental disasters like the thinning of the ozone layer, toxic chemicals, epidemic drug use, and the collapse of the nuclear family. Suppose we talk about the importance of Japanese tourism and Hong Kong immigration to the Canadian economy, about the vital importance of personal computers, and about the unemployment rates of the 1990s. Suppose we tell them our world population is almost double that of the 1960s, and will be over triple by 2025. Would the last three decades of education have been sharply different?

Probably not. Environmentalism scarcely existed as an idea then, let alone as an issue. The idea of our being economically dependent on Asians would have been faintly insulting. The computers of thirty-five years ago were jealously guarded, basement-filling contraptions; students in 1960 certainly couldn't have learned anything about them and wouldn't have gained much if they had. And it's doubtful that the educators of the 1960s would have grasped the reality of ninety million more people every year; certainly we, who have lived through the doubling of the human race, scarcely notice though its impact affects us all.

Suppose we told the educators of 1960 about the effects of crack cocaine, about the frequency of child sexual abuse, about homelessness, about AIDS. Do you think they could have devised and delivered a curriculum to equip the children of the 1960s to deal with such problems, when we ourselves don't know what to do about them?

We don't even have to go back that far. When the high school class of 1994 entered kindergarten in September 1981, Trudeau was in power. Ronald Reagan and Margaret Thatcher were just starting out. Leonid Brezhnev was fighting a hot war in Afghanistan and a cold war with the west. A few doctors were starting to notice a new disease that they would soon call AIDS. Global warming? Ozone loss? That was science fiction. *A billion children were still unborn.*

But if in 1981 I had written a science-fiction novel accurately predicting the last dozen years, I know what my editor would have said:

"The collapse of the Soviet Union in a week, without a nuclear war? Doesn't sound very likely, Crawford. Communist China the fastest-growing capitalist economy in the world? Uh-huh. A war against Iraq using smart bombs, and the Iraqi dictator stays in power? Yeah, right. A separatist party gets over fifty seats in Parliament, and the Tories have just two members left? C'mon, Crawford, give me a break."

We like to kid ourselves that school is to prepare children for something called the real world. We trained the '94 grads to live in a real world that's disappeared before our eyes—and theirs. And for all our education, expertise and confidence, we had no idea what kind of world would replace it.

We did foresee some things. The computer revolution was under way in 1981, and we've tried to prepare the class of '94 for an information economy. In that respect, they're probably ahead of us. But even the kids are probably not ready for the next decade of the computer revolution, as I'll try to show.

The students we lose will be especially unprepared. Many students in the class of '94 dropped out sometime after Grade 8. For one reason or another, about a quarter of the whole class probably didn't graduate. That's very typical; we have lost a quarter to a third of every class for the last thirty years.

Dropouts and non-grads don't have enough resources to cope with change. But change is what they're going to get for the rest of their lives.

The job market will change. Technology will change. The population of Canada will grow older and browner. The uneducated will grow older and poorer. Other than that, it's very hard to say what this country will look like, or need, twenty years from now.

Despite the obvious unpredictability of our world, we educators still take a lot of criticism because we supposedly can't deliver a reliable, predictable product. So we have to give standardized exams that are supposed to prove that the kids have learned some predictable body of knowledge. If we do nothing but teach to the exam, we can cautiously predict that most of our students will get through it. We'd never dare predict that our students would still know the answers five years later—or even five days later.

We might, however, be willing to bet that many of our adult critics would go down in flames on a modern Grade 11 social-studies quiz or Grade 12 math exam. Not only do today's students have more to learn, our generation has had much to unlearn. As Stephen Jay Gould has pointed out in his superb book, *Wonderful Life*, the fossils of the Burgess Shale have overturned not only our original ideas about early life on earth, they have forced us to re-examine our concept of history itself and to accept contingency—uncertainty, unpredictability, chaos—as an inescapable condition of life. The confident vision, having propelled us into ever-increasing scientific knowledge, has also led us back to caution.

I said our adult critics would have trouble with a modern high school exam. But no matter what they've forgotten since school, those adults still function pretty capably in our chaotic world. So do I, even if I did spend my childhood converting pounds and shillings into pence and farthings. The purpose of an education is not to know forever the functions of the cell membrane or the capital of Uruguay. *It is to know how to be a free person who can learn fast in response to the unpredictable.*

Educators are agents of chaos, not of clockwork determinism. By making our students less predictable, we ensure their freedom. We should be proud of ourselves for doing so.

This is not to say we should relax and accept whatever fate has in store for us. Chaos is the opposite of fate. When scientists study chaotic behavior, they soon see unexpected patterns and harmonies in it. While we can't hope to predict the specifics, the trivia, of the future, we can at least look at what helps make the future unpredictable. We can see the broad outlines of potential futures and the forces working to make them real. And depending on how we choose to respond, we as educators can shape the world we want or let others do it for us.

I see three major forces at work in education: demographics, technology, and the political attitudes that arise from the interaction of the first two forces. Before we look to the future, let's consider how the schools have responded to those three forces in the past.

The Rise of the Boomers

When the baby boomers began entering North American schools in the early 1950s, they immediately stressed the system. Schools went on split shifts, hired teachers regardless of training, and threw them into classes of thirty to forty pupils. The provincial governments had no choice but to build more schools and recruit more teachers.

The demand for educators seemed insatiable. Teaching became "what you can always fall back on" for a whole generation of young college students: No matter how incompetent, maladjusted, or weird you were, the beleaguered schools would be quick to hire you. According to a 1980 StatsCan report, teaching absorbed one-third to one-half of all university graduates in the late 1960s and early 1970s.

As the boomer wave rolled through, post-secondary expanded to meet intensifying demand. The universities grew; community colleges sprang up. A whole generation of young academics found careers in these new schools. They were sometimes hard to find, however. In the late 1960s and early '70s, foreign professors tended to dominate the faculties of the new universities and colleges. After some rumbles from Canadian nationalists, a reasonably good professoriat (about thirty percent American and British) was in place by the mid-1970s. It soon settled down to training the next generation of managers for the status quo.

The last of the boomers were born in 1965. Shortly thereafter came a sharp drop in the numbers of newborns; we were into the baby bust, which lasted into the early '80s. By then the boomers were largely finished with formal education and the schools faced an embarrassing set of problems. Once-crowded schools were now empty and echoing. The teachers who had started in the 1950s and '60s were now experienced, highly trained, and relatively well paid. They were also older, but still too far from retirement to make room for newcomers.

Falling enrollments and an aging teaching force combined to make education more expensive than many taxpayers liked. The public was also growing increasingly distant from the schools; by the early 1980s, only about thirty percent of Vancouver households, for example, had school-age children. Adults with no daily contact with the schools tended, in repeated surveys, to be both more critical and less aware of what was going on in education.

The students of the 1980s were the echo boom, children of the boomers. And the boomers, marketers know, are tough customers. As the American marketing demographer Judith E. Nichols has observed in her book *By the Numbers*, boomers are highly competitive, fond of individual attention, and impatient with the very idea of delayed gratification. They want instant results and short, clear explanations of problems that may be complex and obscure. Boomer parents have therefore put some unusual political pressures on the schools.

The schools have tried to respond to boomer parents' desires for more individualized instruction. A generation ago, some students had been "slow" or "inattentive" or "poor readers"; parents and educators alike had seen these as either moral failings or innate weaknesses, and those who displayed them soon left school.

Now, however, students are learning-disabled, or suffering from attention deficits, or struggling with various forms of dyslexia. Flunking such students is misguided because their traits are, at least in the confident vision, remediable. Meanwhile parents of gifted students demanded enriched programs; parents of severely disabled children demanded integration into regular classrooms. Immigrants' children needed training in English as a second language before they could function well.

Regarding education as just another consumer service, boomer parents have demanded more choice in programs, more accountability in the form of standardized tests, and—where possible—the option of private schools. Tax support of private education has made this option increasingly available since the late 1970s.

These demands are not entirely new. In earlier generations the public system had dealt with them by streaming—placing students of roughly similar ability in the same
class, and modifying the curriculum accordingly. This was
administratively convenient since the teacher did not have
to adopt different strategies for different students. But both
research and common sense showed that such streaming
was certain to defeat many students before they had fairly
begun. It was not a matter of bruising their tender egos,
but of telling them that the system did not expect them to
succeed. This self-fulfilling prophecy also ensured that
large numbers of students would leave school as soon as
possible.

An unexpected effect of streaming as I experienced it in
the 1950s was to segregate students not only intellectually
but emotionally. As a student in my school's middle stream,
I associated with my classmates and those in the top stream.
The students in the bottom stream scarcely existed for us,
and we didn't even notice when they disappeared. Nor did
we ever think that the school might have done a better job
with such students if it had challenged them more.

In an economy with plenty of jobs for the unskilled, such
a school system worked reasonably well (though not as well
as nostalgia says it did). You could even argue that the
system was *supposed* to work that way, separating the working-class goats from the middle-class sheep who would go
on to careers in management and the professions.

But technological change in the 1960s, '70s and '80s
made unskilled jobs increasingly rare. Even as critics despaired about the quality of high school graduates' education, it was evident that completion of Grade 12 was
becoming the bare minimum for most jobs. Without real-
izing it, we educators found that our purpose was changing.
We had tried to identify an academic elite by maximizing
the failure rate. Now we had to equip as many students as

possible with as much of an education as possible—to maximize the success rate. This was in harmony with the results-obsessed confident vision of education, but it also appeared to be a starkly objective economic necessity.

So we faced a difficult task by the mid-1980s. With relatively little money, we had to provide individually tailored instruction for a rapidly changing school population which was going out into a world changing even faster. How well have we done, and how well are we likely to do over the next generation?

The answer is that we have done fairly well by the standards of the old resource economy, and very poorly by the emerging standards of a knowledge-based economy. How well we do in future will depend on what kind of society we as a nation choose to live in.

In 1992 about seventy-two percent of all B.C. Grade 12 students graduated. About three females out of four graduated; so did two out of three males. This figure does not include those who for various reasons had dropped out altogether sometime between Grade 8 and Grade 12. Other provincial school systems have done slightly worse or slightly better.

This is no better a completion rate than we were achieving in the 1960s, and somewhat worse than in 1980. But it is not quite as bleak as it looks. Some students, missing only a course or two or taking a little longer to grow up, quietly complete their high school education within a few months of their classmates. Still others eventually return to adult basic education (ABE) programs in local colleges, and may well go on to post-secondary training.

Still, dropping out or failing to graduate does seem a waste of everyone's time and energy. The job market has too many unskilled young people; colleges are pressed enough for space without having to make room for people needing high-school courses; with so small a pool of educated young people, growth into a knowledge-based economy is slow.

And in some cases, failure to learn in school sets a life-long pattern. Employment and Immigration Canada has found that later attempts to train some dropouts do not succeed very well. They no longer know how to learn; they have suffered a kind of intellectual atrophy.

Over the next quarter-century, young people with little to contribute to the economy will become even more of a problem because of the increasing demands of the old. Less than twenty short years from now, the first of the baby boomers will hit sixty-five. But seniors are already changing North America faster than we realize.

A 1991 report by the B.C. Ministry of Finance shows what we can expect here in B.C. *British Columbia Population Forecast 1990–2016* is only an estimate, but it gives us some sense of the social changes we face in the next quarter-century.

The report predicts a rise in B.C.'s population from 3.2 million to 4.7 million between 1989 and 2016. During the same period, the median age of the population will rise from 34.2 to 41.2 years. In other words we will have as many people over age forty-one as under.

That single fact is going to transform our society. In 1952 only one British Columbian in nine was over age sixty-five. Now it's about one in seven. In twenty years, one in six will be over sixty-five. What's more, one in twenty of us will be over eighty. B.C. now supports 12,000 people over the age of ninety. In twenty years that group will grow to 41,000. I expect the proportional growth of the senior population across Canada will be closely similar.

Seniors will be one of the most powerful groups in society, with plenty of time, money, and energy to defend their interests in the political arena. But they're going to be very costly to look after. Many seniors will need increasingly expensive medical care for an increasingly long time. Most will also need housing, recreation, and other services—even education.

To provide those services, our working population will have to be well-educated and prepared to retrain for new careers in a rapidly changing economy. If they are not increasingly productive, everyone's standard of living will fall. In that case, the government will face lower revenues, meaning it will have fewer resources for education. Inadequate education will lower worker productivity still further, dragging living standards even lower.

While this seems self-evident to us, it may seem less so to a society dominated by politically powerful seniors. The percentage of people in their prime working years, twenty-five to sixty-four, will stay a bit above fifty percent. School-agers (including post-secondary students in their early twenties) will shrink slightly over the next twenty years, to less than a quarter of the population.

Somehow we will need the political and financial resources to educate those young people while supporting a growing senior population. The middle generation will have to accept responsibility for both children and old people, even if it means increasing its own sacrifices. But a society dominated by boomers—of any age—is a society looking for quick fixes, not for long-term solutions.

Our low birth rate complicates matters. The young people doing tomorrow's work will not be the grandchildren of tomorrow's seniors. They will be immigrants, many of them from Asia. Without them, says the B.C. ministry forecast, our population would peak at 3.3 million in 2019. Then it would decline, with seniors making up an ever-larger proportion.

Over forty percent of B.C.'s population growth will come from the rest of Canada, while a third will be immigrants from overseas—mostly from countries overcrowded with young people desperate for a better life. We'll urgently need those immigrants, and they in turn

will need government services to help them become productive Canadians. They'll need decent housing and good
schools. (Thanks to the inevitable labour shortage, they
may well have their pick of jobs—including house construction and teaching.)

Again, politically powerful seniors may not be willing to
give up their privileges for the sake of a bunch of foreigners—even if those foreigners are what we'll need to sustain
our retired population.

The baby busters are now in high school, post-secondary, or entry-level jobs. The echo boomers now in grade
school will soon face another problem: a rapidly aging
teaching population.

Teachers as Grandparents

The demographics of today's teaching profession are hard
to argue with. Our teachers are growing older, quitting the
field in growing numbers, and failing to be replaced by
younger men and women. For example, in 1978 thirty-five
percent of Alberta teachers were under thirty-five. In 1988-
89, only eighteen percent were that young. Half of
Alberta's teachers were between thirty-one and fifty a decade ago. In 1988-89, seventy percent were in that age
range. Alberta teachers' average age is 39.2, and they have
an average of over thirteen years' experience in teaching.
By comparison, B.C. teachers' average age is forty-one and
three out of five of us have at least ten years' experience.

We westerners are younger than the Canadian average,
which in 1991 was forty-two. In 1980, twenty percent of
all Canadian teachers were under thirty; in 1990 only
eleven percent were that young. And where thirteen percent were over fifty in 1980, ten years later the figure was
seventeen percent.

A recent report, "Teacher Supply and Demand in British
Columbia to the Year 2011," offers some sense of what
these trends will mean over the next generation. Prepared

for a committee of education stakeholders, the report is encouraging for some regions and alarming for others. It uses a computer model that can have many results, but the general pattern is clear. If we keep the present student-teacher ratio, B.C. will need about 2,500 new teachers a year for the next decade. In the first decade of the 21st century, the annual demand will rise to 2,800. Most will replace teachers who retire, resign, or go on leave.

Surprisingly, these new teachers won't be very young. Of the students who graduate from teacher-training programs, the B.C. Teachers' Federation estimates that about forty percent never enter the profession at all. About forty percent of the rest, as I mentioned, leave teaching within five years. So the schools will recruit older teachers who have decided to return to the classroom—especially part-time. The report notes that part-timers, only two percent of the teaching force in 1966, were seventeen percent in 1991.

Teacher retirements will soar, starting in the late 1990s, but the average age of the profession won't really fall. It's now 42.1; in 2001 it will be 43.5, and in 2011 it will be 42.6.

Rural districts will lose over fifteen percent of their enrollments by 2011. As their teachers retire, they'll be at a severe competitive disadvantage against big-city schools. Relatively cheap housing and a relaxed lifestyle will be their strongest selling points, but small communities that have depended on resource-extraction industries are likely to be permanently depressed and therefore unattractive to potential teachers.

Urban districts will probably see the most turnover, retiring and recruiting large numbers of teachers. Their enrollments will jump nineteen percent by the end of the decade, and almost as much again by 2011.

Demand for new teachers could, of course, drop sharply just by raising class sizes. Teachers would likely resist such

a move with all means possible. Or demand could rise if
districts offered early-retirement packages. Veteran teachers can cost twice as much as rookies, so inducing them to
retire (even with a big lump-sum payoff and several extra
years of pension) can make financial sense. In many cases,
however, districts may actually hire the same veterans back
part-time at entry-level rates, because too few rookies are
available.

While women will make up most of the teaching population, the report says men will probably continue to fill
most administrative jobs. Almost all part-time teachers will
be women. As well, men will continue to dominate the
teaching of science and math, while women stick to subjects
like languages and special needs.

The report points out that the provincial government is
already working to change these conditions. Forgivable
loans will be available to teachers who stay in rural districts.
Mentors for new teachers will try to keep them in the profession, and Victoria is actively recruiting visible minorities.
Whether these efforts to promote the confident vision will
succeed remains to be seen.

Still, schools will see a huge generation gap form between students and aging teachers. Attitudes developed in
the 1950s and '60s may be wildly inappropriate in the Canada of 2010. Teaching philosophies and methods developed
for the 1980s could be archaic, but that won't stop old
teachers from coasting along obliviously.

Since many students will also be immigrants, intercultural understanding will be crucial. But teachers in their
sixties may be reluctant to learn how to deal with the children of yet another foreign culture arriving here. They
may share their retired neighbours' hostility toward foreigners: Poor immigrants will of course "take jobs away
from Canadians," while rich ones will build monster
houses, drive good cars, and otherwise affront conservative
seniors.

The relative lack of newcomers in the profession will also make it hard for politicians to cause change in the system. Newcomers, with no stake in the status quo, are more likely to be in tune with social changes that require schools to change as well. Veterans, insulated by age, salary, and habit, are likely to drag their heels. (B.C. has seen this response already in many teachers' hostility to the Year 2000.) But political battles rarely do much good for the students who are supposedly everyone's chief concern.

Bear in mind that this search for good new teachers will take place simultaneously with the search for good health-care workers, nursing-home staff, and others dedicated to caring for the elderly and ill. And it will take place simultaneously with the search for highly educated, productive workers—especially in knowledge-economy fields that may be prepared to pay much more than schools can. Each sector of our economy will be competing with the others for the best people it can get. And if any sector fails, all the others will risk failure also.

Bear in mind also that teaching the echo boomers will not be a lifetime's occupation. When they have worked their way through the system, enrollments will fall again early in the next century. Many of the new teachers we will have struggled to recruit will then have to go on to other occupations. They will have to teach adaptability to their students; presumably they will possess it themselves.

So these are the demographic prospects for public education over the next couple of decades: a relatively small multi-ethnic student population competing for resources with a relatively large population of seniors while the working population tries to support both of those groups—and itself—in a rapidly changing society. If we don't recognize these realities, all our confident schemes for improving education will be idle talk.

4

Political Factors in Education

In the mid-1980s I believed that the politics of education, at least in British Columbia, was just a matter of voting the cautious rascals out and the confident saviours in. The saviours would promptly increase school budgets, programs would spring up to address every problem, and all would be well. At that point I was still defining the welfare of education as the welfare of its bureaucracy.

In one of the many ironies of the Socred twilight, it was the Vander Zalm government that came to the bureaucracy's rescue. Ex-principal Tony Brummet proved himself the most effective education minister in decades; a non-academic, Stan Hagen, was an ebulliently supportive minister of advanced education. After years of poverty and neglect, the system felt a sudden surge of optimism. The Sullivan Commission produced a clear picture of the state of the schools and what the public wanted from them. Post-secondary expanded—not as rapidly as it needed to, but at least it was headed in what we considered the right direction: more campuses, more funding, more students, more jobs for educators.

We now know that the Vander Zalm government was borrowing heavily to provide this money, and when the

NDP came into power the party soon ended. We might feel sorry for ourselves that Mike Harcourt wasn't going to find more money, but we missed the real point: *Both the Socreds and the New Democrats realized that public support for education was no stronger than it had ever been.* People wanted all the education they could get without having to pay extra taxes for it. By late 1993, only three or four percent of B.C. voters saw education as a priority issue—perhaps a seventh as many as saw jobs as their top concern.

If a government wouldn't dare raise taxes in the good times of the late 1980s, it certainly wasn't going to do so in the recessionary '90s. Still less was it going to borrow any more than the bare minimum the machine needed to keep from stalling altogether.

That minimum somehow kept maximizing itself through the 1980s. According to Statistics Canada, the country spent $48.2 billion on education in 1990-91; that represented an increase of 117 percent over 1980-81, while the Consumer Price Index during the same decade rose only seventy-eight percent. Much of this increase reflects the rapid rise in the student population after years of steady decline in the late 1960s and 1970s; enrollments bottomed out in 1985 and have been climbing ever since. But the public perception is that education spending is out of control and needs severe pruning. Not many politicians want to argue.

So if we are going to do something serious about education, we need to understand much more than the stated policies of the various parties. We need to understand not just the political weather of the day, but the climate that persists for decades. In this chapter I want to look at some of the more vexing problems in that climate.

I mentioned earlier the stark fact that schools, colleges, and universities are major influences on the economies of their communities—both directly as creators of payrolls and indirectly as producers of skilled workers. This is no doubt as it should be, but it means that a very feudal kind of politics sometimes overwhelms pedagogy.

For much of the last century, North American public education served the political requirements of an industrial economy run by middle-class whites of northwest European extraction. As other groups arrived, the schools assimilated some while rejecting others: Italians, Asians, and east European Jews did well, while Hispanics and blacks did poorly. Native Indians, as Canadians have seen in the residential-schools nightmare, suffered severely at the hands of public education.

So assimilation opened doors to some people: they went on to further education, and then into professions where they flourished. Their prosperity gave them political influence, and they tended to take for granted that the system which had benefited them was the only one worth supporting. The politicians they elected certainly reflected that attitude. Theirs was a confident vision; they certainly believed that education would both equip an elite class for the exercise of power and oblige that class to act in the interests of the whole society. The elite's vision, however, did not extend to groups outside itself. For all its meritocratic convictions, the elite honestly didn't think merit existed outside those of northwest European descent.

But even the least advantaged groups produced some political leaders who could demand school reform in the name of the same confident vision. They saw the system as inherently biased against their groups, and called for real equality of opportunity. Among other achievements, such leaders ended racial segregation in the American schools.

The pressure for equal access to education—and therefore to good jobs, high income, and social prestige—has operated over decades if not generations. The results, over the long term, are generally good. Even where equal access has caused problems, they have been a better class of problem than those the old system faced. I'll return to those problems shortly, because they're still very important, but first let's look at a built-in short-term problem: government itself.

The Lasting Problem of Short-Term Solutions

During the school-bashing era of the early 1980s, I felt baffled at how the Social Credit government—in power almost continuously for thirty years—could so unfairly criticize the schools it had created. Didn't the Socreds understand that they themselves were responsible for the state of education? And didn't the voters understand it too?

Eventually I realized the obvious: in the short term, education is politically more useful as a problem than as a solution. Even a dying government can prolong its life by raising the alarm about problems in school: greedy teachers, wasteful school boards, illiterate students. An angry electorate can feel that it's acting to correct the problems by voting for the school critics.

This strategy works in opposition as well: the B.C. New Democrats sat at education's bedside all through the Socred '80s, bewailing the harm done by underfunding and promising a speedy restoration to health. Trusting soul that I was, in my 1985 book *School Wars* I took the NDP at its word and called for its election.

Within a year or so of their eventual accession to power, however, the New Democrats were talking about the folly of "throwing money" at education problems. The Year 2000 program, conceived and implemented during the Vander Zalm years by Tony Brummet, became an orphan; even the groups who had backed it, like the B.C. Teachers' Federation, now proclaimed themselves still in favor of "education reform," but not necessarily of the Year 2000.

In the fall of 1993 Premier Mike Harcourt proclaimed the Year 2000 Document a failure and fired Education Minister Anita Hagen and Advanced Education Minister Tom Perry. A new round of school-bashing started off,

mercifully not including the government this time. Ironically, the bashers were the right-wingers, supporters of the
Vander Zalm Socreds who had come up with the Year
2000.

Once more we faced the prospect of short-term solutions to long-term problems, and—as usual—the prospec-
tus was a government paper on education reform.

Education-reform reports are a form of genre fiction,
like Harlequin romances or spy novels. People like genre
fiction because it offers predictable thrills and wish-fulfill-
ment fantasy. It never looks seriously at the problems it
pretends to deal with. The same is true of the education-
reform report. Art Charbonneau, the new education minister, became the latest author in this genre in November
1993 when he released "Improving the Quality of Education in B.C."

His report is one in a long series going back to the Kidd
Report in the 1930s. Other classics include the Chant
Commission in 1960, Brian Smith's report in 1981, Jack
Heinrich's *Let's Talk About Schools* in 1984, and the 1987
Sullivan Commission report that led to the Year 2000.

All these reports have familiar characters—the Groaning
Taxpayer, the Concerned Parent, the Evil (but Brilliant)
Foreign Competitor, the Poor Dumb Student. Teachers
are Saintly Drudges, Lazy Fatcats or Leftist Nitwits. Like
a Tom Clancy techno-thriller, every education-reform report warns that the Fate of the Nation is at stake. Once
schools had to save us from the Communist Menace. Now
the enemies are assorted Asians, who are all better capital-
ists than we are.

Like spy novels, the education-reform report often fea-
tures a Secret Weapon. Sometimes it's whole language and
child-centered education. Sometimes it's phonics and back-
to-basics. If the Good Guys can only use the Secret
Weapon, they'll save us all.

Charbonneau clearly aimed his product at a market that wanted letter grades, standard exams, and not much consistency. For example, he said students by Grade 10 should have "advanced ability in English, mathematics, science and social studies." That would be a neat trick when even today's college students (and some BA's) need remedial spelling and grammar. He also wanted "more rigorous" grad requirements and "improved standards"—while still somehow reducing the number of dropouts.

Charbonneau rightly included computer literacy as a basic skill, but backed away from funding more high-tech in the schools. He told me in an interview that maybe, through co-op programs, teachers and students could learn about computers by contacts with private businesses. Well, sometimes science fiction does come true.

He ignored some inconvenient problems. By 1993 many school districts, including Vancouver, were facing a financial disaster far worse than anything in the Socred era or Stephen King's horror novels. Budget cuts and teacher layoffs would make it tough to provide students with "learning assistance, extra time, different material or a different form of instruction," as Charbonneau promised.

His report predicted "a prosperous and fulfilled future" to well-educated people. But he admitted in our talk that a good education no longer guarantees a good job. The best he seemed to hope for was that educated, job-hungry young people would attract foreign investment. In other words, other countries would keep the economic initiative. We would just have to hope they considered B.C. worth saving.

This is the premise of a romance novel—if only we're attractive enough, some day our prince will come. A nuts-and-bolts engineer like Art Charbonneau (in a socialist party, no less) should have realized that he was peddling a pretty forlorn right-wing fantasy.

Well, fantasy is what the electorate usually goes for, and it's what the politicians offer because they see no point in working for the long term. That explains why they consistently underfund education even though they know that education is literally a hot investment.

One American economist, Barry Bluestone, calculates that for every dollar the state of Massachusetts invests in post-secondary education, it gets back a dollar and fifty-seven cents in increased tax revenues. On an annual basis, Massachusetts is earning between eight and nine percent on its post-secondary investment. Comparable returns doubtless come from public education as well—and of course the schools make post-secondary education possible. So, far from being a drain on the state, education is actually subsidizing the state. (However, as I'll try to show later, we could probably get the same return for a smaller investment by abandoning our fetish for credentials.)

Why, then, are governments cutting post-secondary and public education budgets instead of pumping every available nickel into them? It's not because politicians are stupid. They're just shortsighted. From the politicians' point of view, the current government, whoever it happens to be, gets praise for keeping expenses down, not for generating future revenue. Why should the government care if well-educated citizens will pay more income tax and sales tax over their working lives? That money will benefit only future governments, not the present one.

New Politics, Old Structures
Many of the furious conflicts in education are attempts to reconcile the old system with the new. We recognize that all children deserve a good education, and that we can't afford to give them a bad one because we're going to depend on them to support us in our long old age. So we try all kinds of new approaches to maximize success:

integration of special needs children, program continuity and continuous progress, portfolio assessment, individualized education plans. These are the approaches of the confident vision, more intent on results than on processes.

But we still try to do all this in classrooms designed to separate sheep from goats and flunk the goats (or worse yet, to call the goats "sheep in progress"). We expect one teacher, with perhaps an assistant or two, to do wonders when the class includes an emotionally disturbed child, three to five children who speak little English, a couple of children from abusive families, two kids who are so bright they're "severely gifted," and a couple of learning-disabled kids. And we expect the teacher to deliver a results-based curriculum through good old full-frontal teaching: an adult standing and talking to quiet, attentive children.

As a teacher, I'm not ashamed of what we're doing badly; I'm proud that we're doing as well as we are with the resources we're given. But we could do better if the political climate supported serious education. Instead, the climate encourages attitudes that would be funny if they didn't do so much harm to children.

The Representative Fallacy
Educators with the confident vision sometimes display the vices of their virtues. We remember, with shame and embarrassment, the racism and sexism of our own school years. We realize that we never really noticed our classmates who dropped out; they were in a different stream anyway—the dumb stream—and we certainly wouldn't have socialized with kids like them. Most of today's teachers, after all, were children who flourished under the old maximum-failure system. It was in our interest to identify with the system, not with its rejects. In a hideously ironic reaction against our earlier privileged condition, we have swung far over to the opposite side: Now we are willing

to assign privilege to anyone who is in a group that once suffered discrimination. It's funny, in a morbid way. But it's also as dangerous as sniffing gasoline.

Call it the "representative fallacy." Springing from the confident vision, it argues that every group in society ought to appear in proportional numbers everywhere. In every profession, every legislature, every activity. So if fifty-two percent of Canadians are women, then fifty-two percent of Parliament should be women. Otherwise, Parliament will fail to "represent" them. If an ethnic group is rare in a profession, it isn't "represented"—as if the profession were a kind of Parliament also.

All kinds of professions—law, architecture, teaching—are under fire from "equity groups" who feel their members are too rare in those occupations. Many governments, both here and in the U.S., are demanding better "representation" in such professions. For the schools, this demand means granting special status to people because of their ancestry or their sex or the particular set of disabilities they must deal with.

The fallacy relies on opposing assumptions. One assumption is that everyone is exactly equal in abilities, interests, and attitudes. Only the present power elite keeps some people from succeeding in particular fields. So if Inuit women rarely become architects and surgeons, it's because architects and surgeons are sexist, racist bigots. The second assumption directly contradicts the first. It says your race, sex, and ethnicity make you utterly different from everyone else. So no one can represent your interests except someone just like you.

Representation in high-income, high-prestige occupations is the only kind we worry about. No one complains about the absence of women among garbage collectors and fur trappers. No one thinks more Chinese and Scandinavians should join the ranks of welfare recipients.

We're perfectly right to want people of all kinds to seek

careers without regard for race, sex or ethnicity. But we're worse than wrong to push for "representative" numbers in all high-status occupations and the education programs that lead to such occupations.

So we want representative numbers of blacks in law or medicine? Should we demand representative numbers of whites in pro basketball? Should we insist on Jewish and Muslim representation in the pork producers' association? And once we've hired a representative number from a particular "equity group," should we turn away all additional applicants from that group?

In a society that really cared only about individual ability, we wouldn't mind if all the dentists happened to be Haitian grandmothers, all the teachers were Sikhs in wheelchairs, and all the MPs were Native Indians or Doukhobors. Our only concern would be whether they could do their jobs.

The fallacy lures us into misunderstanding the nature of democracy. It encourages us to regard society as a treasury to plunder, not as a community to support. But the really dangerous aspect of the fallacy is that it entrenches the discrimination it pretends to attack. It says that the most important thing about you is something you can't control—something you were born with. That's what should determine your job, your status, your privileges. That, in brief, is a definition of racism, sexism, classism. For an educator brought up in the confident vision, this is the revenge of a cruel but witty God.

In the schools, the representative fallacy threatens to roll back half a century of struggle for equality. Some of our colleagues tell us, with straight faces, that minority children need role models who have the same skin colour, or who are the same sex, or who come from the same culture. Our colleagues go on to say that the curriculum doesn't "represent" such children because it deals with a "Eurocentric" literary canon, or with history as the actions of dead white males, or with an approach to scholarship that alienates women. Whatever the complaint, the unspoken premise is that victimized minorities are so limited in their mental powers that they can relate to nothing but their fellow-victims: a breathtaking insult to people who have enough problems with their enemies, never mind their friends.

I'll have more to say about this genteel-fascist perversion of egalitarianism later. For now let us bear in mind that it is one more major problem in trying to strengthen the ties between confident educators and an increasingly cautious public. And those ties need to be stronger than ever.

Educating Through The Media

I'm assuming that you're reading this book because—as a parent or an educator—you want to take an active and constructive role in improving the schools. Even if you're a hardshell conservative dedicated to the cautious vision, you think you can act—alone and with others—to improve the schools and therefore improve society. If you're a confident-vision liberal, you know that education is the key to a better society. Whether or not you agree with my view of the bureaucracy, you think education can work better for more people at lower cost if the public takes an active, informed role in running the schools.

So I'm going to address you directly instead of resorting to an impersonal "we" or "concerned citizens." Much of what I have to say has to do with disaster control; that's because one disastrous incident can undo years of effort. It can be even worse if you haven't put years of effort into creating strong ties between schools and the public they serve.

A few years ago I gave a talk in Winnipeg to members of CACE, the Canadian Association of Communicators in Education. They're the school-district PR people who crank out the press releases and organize the press conferences. My talk was really a kind of workshop on how to deal with various kinds of education horror stories: nutty parents, tragic children, idiotic principals, demented trustees, rabid teachers—the works. The idea was to get the PR people to think about such problems before they hit, and to work out some basic principles for solving them.

I later learned that the response of the PR people from Alberta ran something like this: It was a lot of fun, but we don't need that kind of preparation. *These things don't happen to us.* That, of course, was before Ralph Klein became premier in 1993 and began hacking school budgets to bits. This attitude is still a stubbornly wishful part of bureaucratic school culture, and one reason why that culture is in such trouble.

B.C.'s reality in education has been over a decade of misfortune, and to some extent we educators have been responsible for it. Part of my purpose here is to help make sure your schools escape what others have been going through. And I also want to suggest how the ways we use the media are likely to affect our schools and even our society.

Maybe we just don't live right in B.C. For example, since I gave that talk in Winnipeg, the Vancouver School Board's PR guy has had to deal with one disaster after another—for years. A high-school student, signing a friend's yearbook, was accidentally run over and killed by another student on school property. Teachers have called more strikes than a baseball umpire. AIDS has become a major issue. Perverts have tried to kidnap little girls out of elementary-school washrooms. The school-board chairman said in public that photocopying copyrighted textbooks is okay, high-school principals are fighting a guerilla war against youth gangs, kids are coming to class hungry and abused, and a host of other nightmares are besetting B.C. schools—all of them far worse than the nightmares I tried to describe in my talk. If you think they don't happen in your schools as well, you have much to learn.

Taken one by one, these horror stories are mere episodes. Taken all together, they can create a devastating image of education in the minds of the public. When they come at a time of economic and political unrest, they can be used to justify catastrophic political interference in the schools, interference that can make matters even worse.

I don't think a school system in North America is immune to political attack, and I know that a few public-relations officials will not be enough to defend the schools when the attack comes. Everyone in the system—teachers, administrators, trustees, parents—should be ready to defend the schools. Otherwise, education will suffer from the corruption and waste that we in B.C. have come to call school wars—a permanent state of distrust and confrontation between educators and government.

Any public enterprise, like education, reflects the public's consensus or lack of consensus, and it can go only in the directions the public decides. If you think, therefore, that politics can be kept out of education, you are not only wrong, you are asking for trouble. You're asking for a school war.

If B.C.'s experience is typical, a school war needs a few volatile elements thrown together and then shaken. The first of these is an aging population, with only a small proportion of young adults with school-age children. Older voters are a menace in a couple of ways: first, they no longer have children who can benefit from schooling, and second, they tend to disapprove of whatever the schools are doing at the moment.

This isn't surprising. As I observed earlier, we like to flatter our own education by criticizing our children's. We look back at our schooling with ruthlessly selective memories, editing out the boredom, the complacency, the sheer pointlessness and error of much of what we were taught. We certainly forget that in our time, our elders despaired of us. Then, when we gain some vague sense of what's going on in today's schools, we're righteously appalled. So a growing number of older voters, watching their school taxes rise every year, can become alienated from education. Politicians listen to the muttered complaints, and consider ways of answering them.

The education community, therefore, has two sets of problems—the real problems of the real schools, which we deal with every day, and the perceived problems of the perceived schools, which the public worries about. We won't get very far with the real problems until the public perception of the schools is close to ours. So we have a triple task: to educate our students; to educate our community; and to educate ourselves. For all three tasks we must educate through the media.

In my first year as a school trustee in North Vancouver, I winced to see that we had budgeted something like $40,000 for public relations. What a waste, I thought. Propaganda money that could've gone to better use in the classroom. I soon learned otherwise, and I learned it the hard way by suffering a sound defeat when I ran for re-election. The public literally did not know what was going on in the schools, so it responded to our recession and the Socred restraint propaganda out of fear and ignorance and a desire to make somebody else suffer too.

I expect I would have been defeated even if we'd doubled our PR budget. By then the damage was done. Good public relations is like fire insurance: you must have it long before the need arises, and by the early '80s the smell of smoke was getting strong.

Now, all school districts pay some attention to PR. We like to get our scholarship winners into the local paper, and it doesn't hurt to have a top football team. School principals send home newsletters, and parent groups are usually encouraged to work closely with school staff. That's fine as far as it goes, but it's mostly preaching to the converted—to the parents who know and understand what we're trying to do. To the rest of the community, the schools scarcely exist.

If you're an educator like my B.C. colleagues, you think this is just dandy. You regard the media as essentially un-interested in good news, and you regard good news as the only kind the schools should disseminate. You cringe at the thought of your school being involved in some kind of scandal, with TV cameramen swarming onto the school grounds and angry parents snarling about how this outrage could have been prevented, whatever it was, if only the schools were doing their job.

As an educator who is also in the media, I can tell you that you get what you give. A hostile attitude to the media will guarantee that only hostile stories about education will reach the public.

I didn't realize this myself until after I lost the election. Like many another discredited politician, I went straight to the media and began writing a weekly column on edu-cation. Pretty soon I noticed something that surprised me. Other members of the media began coming to me for some kind of handle on what was going on, and I learned that they were as pig-ignorant on education issues as the rest of the public.

Moreover, they were paranoiacally suspicious of all sides in the controversy, and determined not to be deceived by anyone. So their coverage tended to the simple-minded and the trivially "balanced." They showed a talking head saying the government was terrible, and then they showed another talking head saying the government was trying to be "fair and equitable." They showed a news reporter standing in a schoolyard with a microphone, saying both sides were digging in. And that was it.

When I teach my students about resumés and job inter-views, I like to talk about "employer anxiety." That's the dread any employer feels about choosing the wrong person for the job, and it leads employers to hire two kinds of people: the people who somehow managed not to provoke employer anxiety, and the people who deliberately prevented that anxiety by being known to the employer already.

In China, I learned another word for it: *guanxi*. It means connections, relationships, and it's the only way China can get around its own bureaucracy. You know somebody who knows somebody, and you can do each other some favors. The whole country is a web of informal allegiances and support groups, and woe betide the person who lacks *guanxi* because no one is going to come to his aid.

We need, as parents and educators, to start developing our own *guanxi* with the media, and through them with the non-parent public. And we have to do it before the scandal hits, before the politician decides to exploit us, before the public gets scared again about rising school costs.

I suggest, therefore, that educators should take the initiative by bringing the media into the schools, and showing reporters what's really going on. It might work something like this. The school board or teachers' association invites a local TV station news team to drop around for some background information. The reporters are enticed perhaps with the prospect of a free lunch and some good human-interest footage in the local high-school cafeteria.

They meet the local trustees, the executive of the teachers' association, the principal of the high school. They get some straight talk from their hosts. We've got this problem, we've got that problem, but we've also got some programs going here that are making a real difference in kids' lives. The hosts can supply some solid facts and figures on such issues as dropout rates, the demands of handicapped students, the percentage who go on to college, the skills of the teaching staff, the strange and terrible mysteries of education finance.

This will accomplish a couple of useful things. It will give the reporters your names and faces, and a chance to get to know you as people, not just as mouthpieces for this or that interest group after a crisis has already arisen. You can give them at least a rough sense of how the system operates these days, how it's changed over the last few years, and where it seems to be going. And it will also give you the names and faces of people in the media, who will no longer seem quite as sinister. All of these accomplishments will sharply reduce media anxiety about education, and vice versa.

Educators who take this simple step will soon discover that they and the media have some interests in common: both want a good story—factual, vivid, and lively. It doesn't have to be a bad-news story, although sometimes a bad-news story is just what you want. It can put pressure on the powers that be to solve a problem. You and the media aren't antagonists now, but associates who have developed some trust and mutual respect.

Now, if you want good stories about education in the media, you have to know what the media's needs are—their deadlines, their news policies, their economic limitations. Be assured that your guests will be glad to inform you on these and other topics, sometimes at great length. Listen sympathetically. That's what friends are for. Among other things, you may also get an earful about what school critics are telling the media, and much of it will be painfully accurate.

If you are a typical confident-vision educator, you may try to discredit the critics by damning them as ignorant, malevolent, or both. If you are a wise educator, you will tell the media that the critics have valid concerns and you share them—but you're trying to deal with those concerns in practical, day-to-day ways. (By the same token, if you're a disgruntled cautious-vision parent or taxpayer, the media will mistrust you if you damn and blast all educators and fail to give them credit for brains and concern.)

In addition, you should give the media an idea of

potential stories for the future: an important round of negotiations, a new safety program, a crucial vote. Explain why these are important not only to education but to the community, and express your views in the context of the good of the community, not just the good of your organization. (Again, a naïve believer in the confident vision may invoke superior educator knowledge and come across looking like an arrogant twit.)

The media will be grateful for tips about future events; people in the news business are amazingly unhappy about surprises, and would much prefer to know in advance when news is on the way. In some cases, you may be able to strengthen your media relations by supplying an exclusive story, but do so judiciously because you don't want to alienate your other contacts.

Be prepared to give the same crash course over and over again, as new reporters, often young and ignorant, are assigned to cover you. A reporter who doesn't understand the background of a story is a reporter who will go for a simple-minded angle. And that will surely distort the story and the public's understanding of it.

You will find that you acquire a new aura among your media contacts. You are no longer a *target*, someone to be pestered into confessing your crimes. Instead, you are a *source*, someone who's got the inside dope. And that is a very agreeable thing to be, I can assure you. Journalists presume that targets lie with every breath they take. Sources are veritable oracles of truth and wisdom.

This fact of media life was confirmed for me once after the B.C. provincial government announced a new funding policy based on taxpayer referenda. I published a long and negative story about the policy in the Sunday *Province*. The next day I got a call from a TV reporter who raised no serious arguments against my position. He then came to interview me and ran my comments on the air without contradiction. For him, I was a source. And I'll continue to be a source for my media colleagues until I compromise myself in some way on a story. If I ever do, I'll be just another target and I'll have only myself to blame.

Life with the media will never be all sweet romance. You must expect criticism now and then. It will be extremely unpleasant, especially when it's justified. If you feel the media have ill-used you, bite your tongue. Loud and abusive complaints will get you nowhere, and will make your critics smirk with pleasure at having gotten under your skin. When they've misquoted you, or distorted the facts as you see them, let the media know, calmly and factually, without reproach, and conclude on a positive note. I speak from experience here; where I have got a fact wrong, and my target has let me know it quietly and privately, it has been like coals of fire on my head.

Media relations, in other words, are much like conjugal relations. As long as you have to go on living together, it is in your own interest to get along agreeably despite any number of petty annoyances, conflicts, and misunderstandings.

If you adopt a constructive attitude toward the media, you are a long way toward securing a strong base of public support, but don't expect overnight success. You are now embarked on a long-term propaganda campaign, designed to change or strengthen attitudes over months and years. (And by propaganda I don't mean misleading the public. On the contrary, the best propaganda advice I can give you is to tell the truth, tell it well, and tell it often. Even when it's bad news. Especially when it's bad news.)

No one's going to become a solid supporter of the schools after just one story about a star teacher or a likable scholarship winner. But as such stories come week after week, month after month, the public begins to realize that the system seems to be running pretty well. To offer another example, if you've got a homework-hotline show on your local cable station, the public will begin to respect the level of course work you're demanding, and the skill with which you explain difficult concepts.

The test comes with a crisis, when you've got to switch to "shock" propaganda. The system is at risk; a threat is looming, and now you must mobilize the public to defend the schools. It is the propaganda that comes before an election campaign, or some other crucial public decision.

That was the problem we faced in B.C. a few years ago when the Minister of Education actually fired three school boards—including Vancouver's—for resisting budget cutbacks. The school boards had been elected by the public, but their long-term propaganda had not been operating long enough to overcome our adversaries' propaganda. Even in Vancouver, with its brilliantly run public-awareness campaign, five months was not enough time to build a solid base of active public support for the board's anti-cutbacks position.

You may say that in hindsight it didn't matter; when the minister finally withdrew his appointed administrators, the anti-cutbacks trustees were swept back into office in a landslide. Yes, but remember that the landslide was a function of building a good political machine, not of building a broad base of support. A year later the anti-cutbacks group was reduced to a small minority on the board, and a minority it remained thereafter.

So broad support for the schools is what Canadian educators and parents must have if they are not to repeat our unhappy experience. That experience might be summed up in the comment made to me during the restraint era by a superintendent in one of the best districts in the province. "I haven't made an educational decision since I took over this job," he said. Instead, he'd been deciding what programs he could most expeditiously cut, which teachers he should let go, which fires he should put out. His job had become not education leadership, but damage control; it may have contributed to his untimely death.

Don't assume that I'm arguing solely for a PR-based, mass-manipulating scheme for conning the public. A con game won't work; you've got to have a good product as well as a good ad campaign. Good media relations are a crucial part of educating the public, but not the only part. A real *guanxi* network should extend into the whole community.

For example, trustees, teachers, and parent groups should aggressively seek out other groups. Your local trustees, teachers, and senior administrators should be permanent fixtures at Chamber of Commerce meetings, service organization meetings, trade-union meetings, and meetings of local constituency organizations of all parties. (That's really important—the most dangerous attacks on the schools come from governments, and if the grassroots are alienated from education, the politicians will feel free to abuse you.) Obviously, you'll sometimes be at odds with your fellow-stakeholders, but you should be able to find plenty of common ground. We're talking about long-term concerns here, not this year's spat between teachers and trustees or parents.

Educators should also be learning from the groups they speak to. The business community usually has a few bones to pick with the schools. Listen carefully, and give your business critics frank answers. Just because they're in business doesn't mean they're automatically on the bigoted end of the cautious vision—and even if they are, they deserve a clear and honest account rather than moralizing sermons. The trade unions have their concerns as well; listen, and show how the schools are trying (or failing) to address those concerns. Go to the professional associations, the doctors, lawyers, architects, engineers, and scientists, and hear their views; then explain to them how the modern education system is running and what it needs to serve them better. Again, you won't make many instant converts, but you'll get a respectful hearing and more support than you may expect.

A school system that goes to its community regularly to build and maintain its *guanxi* network is a school system much less likely to suffer sudden rejection or attack. Educators who listen to their community—not just to the parents, but everyone—are going to be much more a part of that community, with a role the community understands and appreciates. In turn, educators will be able to do a better job because they'll understand their community better than before.

Perhaps this sounds like a hell of a lot of work, and you already have so much marking and preparation to do that you can't imagine making it to Chamber of Commerce lunches or Rotary meetings. Maybe the whole idea of *guanxi* offends your ruggedly individualistic soul. But look at B.C. if you want to see what happens without such *guanxi*. Educating your community is just a cost of doing business as a parent or teacher. If you aren't prepared to do so, you're making life harder for your children. If you are prepared to educate your community, you will serve your children better than you ever imagined possible.

Conflict of Interest: Academic Racketeering

Another political problem for education is an embarrassing one for me. We pay a high price for public apathy toward local politics: real-estate agents and developers sit on our municipal councils and disrupt our neighbourhoods in the name of development. And our school boards, because the public doesn't take enough interest in them, often fall prey to educators who are in a blatant conflict of interest. I know; I used to be in it myself.

The people I'm talking about are school-board employees and their spouses, who also serve as school trustees. They don't serve in their own districts, of course. But if you teach in Vancouver while living in Delta, for example, you're perfectly free to serve on the Delta school board. So is your spouse. That means you're in a position to influence your own salary and working conditions. If as a trustee you vote to pay Delta teachers a whacking great increase (and no doubt they deserve it), your fellow-teachers in Vancouver will immediately demand a similar raise.

Legally you're not in a conflict of interest, but in ethical terms you certainly are, as I was when I served as a North Vancouver trustee from 1980 to 1982. Until 1977 I'd been technically an employee of the North Vancouver board, which had paid part of my college's budget. Then the province took over all college funding. That freed college employees to run for school board, and I did. When opponents raised the conflict-of-interest issue, I shrugged it off. After all, real-estate agents and developers serve on municipal councils. And if the law allowed me to serve, why shouldn't I?

But my opponents had been right. I even served on my board's bargaining committee, which quickly reached a settlement with North Van teachers. That settlement, I knew, would be a factor in the settlement my college would make with my faculty association.

I still thought my own obvious fairness and decency exempted me from conflict of interest. After all, we'd settled with our teachers for what turned out to be the provincial average that year. And everything I did was perfectly legal. Like Vander Zalm, I found it easy to believe what was most convenient. And like him, I confused what was legal with what was ethical. But by any objective standard my decisions helped to influence my own income and working conditions.

Should I have simply abstained from voting on such decisions? Quite a few teacher-trustees do just that, but they short-change their voters. Trustees ought to be able to do 100 percent of the job.

Many teachers, professors, and employees of educational institutions now serve on our school boards. They do good work, and they do it to improve the schools—not to line their own pockets. But they're on the wrong side of the table. Even the potential for conflict of interest ought to disqualify a person for public service. That would mean no educator, or educator's spouse, could serve on a school board.

And no real-estate agent or developer could serve on a municipal council.

Dealing with School Violence

For many reasons, the political climate has grown increasingly hostile to public education since the early 1980s. John Kenneth Galbraith—a strong proponent of the confident vision—has identified the problem as "the culture of contentment," in which the contented are determined to stay that way no matter what cost their contentment may impose on others less well off. The contented, in turn, see Galbraith as just another confident pickpocket using their money to subsidize the idleness of the poor.

The division has worsened over the last decade. Overt racism is more common, the poor feel less in control of their lives than ever, and the affluent feel they have discharged their civic duty by donating to their local food bank—one of the few growing organizations in the recessionary 1990s.

In a climate of malaise, the weather often turns violent. And when it does so in school, the education bureaucracy finds itself in an increasingly hopeless predicament. In 1988, 11,385 young Canadians were charged with crimes of violence under the Criminal Code. In 1989 the number rose to 19,580. By 1991 the number charged was down to 18,769. That was still far too high, and grim proof that youth violence is no figment of the media's imagination.

Educators have been taking effective steps to head it

off—at least on their own turf. But they will remain on the defensive as long as the larger society fails to provide decent working and living conditions for the million Canadian children who live in poverty, and for their parents.

Burnaby schools have been notably active in dealing with violent behaviour, and districts across Canada are benefiting. In the late 1980s Burnaby adopted a zero-tolerance policy on weapons, but that was just the first step. The district went on to ban positive portrayals of violence in school materials, extended the definition of weapons to include anything used to harm or threaten anyone, and forbade any kind of physical violence, threats or intimidation. Mitch Bloomfield, a former police officer, has helped to develop and implement these policies as Burnaby's co-ordinator of youth services.

"The issue affects every kid," says Bloomfield, "but fewer than five percent of youth are directly involved in serious violence."

Bloomfield has helped to develop Burnaby's Youth Violence Resource Information Project, funded by the Attorney General, which surveyed Canada and the U.S. for programs that prevent youth violence. The project has compiled a collection of useful materials, and has sent out a catalogue of those materials to all B.C. school districts.

Interest doesn't stop there. "We're getting requests from coast to coast," says Bloomfield. The project serves as a lending library, sending out material to districts all over Canada.

Bloomfield sees four answers to youth violence. First, kids need to learn pro-social communication skills at an early age—including how to manage anger. Second, schools must develop programs that show kids the negative results of gang involvement. Third, the whole community has to work against violence—parents, students, police, social services, the schools. Fourth, schools have to develop strict weapons and safety policies.

But teen violence was a cliché even in the 1950s era of rebels without a cause and blackboard jungles. Are we over-reacting? Bloomfield doesn't think so. "We're seeing serious violence at a younger age," he says. "And now groups are involved, not one-on-one but fifteen against one or two."

And why is it happening? Bloomfield sees kids who are alienated from their families and society. TV and videos have desensitized children until they simply don't realize what harm they're doing. Social stress and less sense of connection to other people can lead to violence.

Restoring that connection is a major part of Burnaby's anti-violence program. A student advisory committee tells the district's school board what kids are thinking, and the students can generate agenda items for the board. Another teen committee helps to plan recreation services in Burnaby.

Like Burnaby, districts all over B.C. are working to stop violence before it starts, and to deal firmly with anyone who hurts, threatens or intimidates students. The B.C. Teachers' Federation is also tackling the issue, involving parents and children as well.

These are admirable steps, and they certainly head off a great deal of trouble. Nevertheless, they are dealing with symptoms rather than causes. The larger society, feeling as stressed as it does, is in no mood for deep analysis—least of all of its own failures. Instead the cry goes up for more punishment, stiffer sentences, a Young Offenders Act with more teeth in it. No doubt some young criminals should indeed go to jail for long periods, if only to keep them away from other children. For others, increased punishment only aggravates the offender's problems without creating a more secure society.

For our purposes here, the punitive public attitude limits what educators can do. We can and should make our schools safe places, but every dollar we spend to do so will have to come out of some other part of the education budget. Every hour we spend checking lockers for weapons or sorting out the aftermath of a fight will come out of the time we can give to actual teaching. When schools become beleaguered garrisons, they cease to be very effective schools; the American experience shows us abundant proof of that.

Let us consider what the education bureaucracy might do, in its fighting retreat, to make school more humane and therefore more worth defending in the first place.

5

A Curriculum For a
Healthy Society

What we teach and learn is always a reflection of the political and cultural climate. As a boy in Mexico, I gained a particular interpretation of the Mexican-American War that was sharply different from that in the American curriculum. (At least the Americans paid some attention to Mexico; Canada got, as I recall, a couple of weeks in Grade 10 social studies.) The statesmen of one era are the oppressive dead white males of another. One generation's culture hero is the next generation's drunken bum. And what one generation knows as a matter of simple literacy is so much Trivial Pursuit to the next.

I'm neither willing nor qualified to discuss every topic in today's curriculum, nor to assess it in the light of yesterday's glories and tomorrow's needs. We would soon bog down in nostalgia ("Gee, I *loved* Latin and diagramming sentences") or intense but transient anxieties ("If the kids don't all learn computer spreadsheets, the West is doomed").

Curriculum falls under the "schooling" category of "know that." Obviously students need to know a lot, and the process seems to work better when they do so in a systematic, incremental way. But it also involves "know why," a whole attitude toward learning that becomes self-sustaining after formal education ends.

We simply cannot teach everything that everyone would like us to. Whenever a social problem arises and people say, "Only education can solve it," that's the confident vision talking—the belief that schools are indoctrination centres that can program smiling, sensitive New Age citizens who will tolerate anything and anyone except those wicked old problems and those oppressive patriarchs who create the problems in the first place. With so many educators also holding the confident vision, the schools too often think they actually can create such fantasy-citizens and a fantasy-Utopia for them to live in.

So into the finite time we give to education we must squeeze spelling rules and AIDS information, calculus and environmental politics, medieval history and anger management, Native studies and computer science, social responsibility and entrepreneurial values.

This is a self-defeating process. If the problem is going to be part of the curriculum, someone has to design the curriculum, create materials, show teachers how to implement it, and assess how well the students have mastered it. This creates new opportunities for bureaucratic empire builders who require non-classroom office space, access to secretarial and desktop-publishing staff, computers and faxes, and a budget permitting attendance at conferences and retreats every few weeks. Teachers who would rather deal with adults than children (and thereby enjoy more income and prestige) gravitate readily to this career shift.

Nevertheless, the curriculum will change whether we like it or not, and will do so in response to political and cultural pressures. Educators should be ready to encourage some curriculum trends while resisting others as strenuously as possible. Their criteria should be simple:

- Does teaching this subject, in this manner, with these materials, to these children, foster further learning in this and related disciplines?

- Does it have an application in the workplace, in cultural activities, or in the maintenance of health and fitness?
- Does it foster a sense of civic responsibility and capability? If so, does it do so by encouraging logical thought, not by emotional manipulation?
- Does it give children the basics for an informed opinion on issues related to the subject?

If all answers are yes, the subject deserves consideration; if any answers are no, the subject at best deserves retention as an optional field of study where time, resources, and student interest permit it.

We never know enough. As a high-school teacher of mine once pointed out, the more we learn the more aware we become of the scale of our ignorance. A little later I'll look at what kind of curriculum students could profitably learn in the early 21st century, but first I'd like to look at the function of just one part of the present curriculum: the arts. They have suffered serious neglect in recent years, and have paid a heavier social price for that neglect than we realize. The arts are symptomatic of problems that ultimately threaten both the cautious and the confident visions.

Why Education Needs The Arts And The Arts Need Education

For the artist, art provides a means of self-definition: I am the one who sings or paints or dances or writes, as distinct from other people who plant or build or dig or fight. (Of course, farmers or carpenters can sing or paint as well, and by doing so they further define themselves as particular kinds of farmers or carpenters. In America, the singing cowboy has enjoyed a special celebrity. In Canada, it's the singing Mountie, which tells you something about the differences between the two nations.)

Self-expression is another function of the arts. It's not just that I sing songs or play the kazoo, but that I sing and play in a special way that puts my own personal stamp on the material. This is true even of artistic traditions that emphasize doing things exactly as they've always been done: the artist then displays how he or she, specifically, does things the way they've always been done. Complete self-effacement within the performing arts is just another form of self-advertisement.

Exerting influence over others is a third function. We sometimes think of the artist as an isolated individual, toiling in some lonely garret to produce magnificent novels or paintings, or practicing a dance step over and over in some deserted studio. This stereotype is particularly strong in western countries, which have a romantic tradition of glorifying the artist as an individual.

But art has no real function at all if it isn't social, if it isn't a means of communicating with—and thereby influencing—other people. The nature of such communication depends to a great extent on our state of mind, on the degree of consciousness we bring to the act of communication. Northrop Frye, who was one of Canada's greatest literary critics and scholars, makes a very useful distinction that we should keep in mind. He defines the *self* as the individual engaged in communication with others; the *ego* is the individual engaged in an occasionally interrupted monologue that has no purpose except to express the ego and its various conditions. The self cares passionately about other people and its relationships to them; the ego cares nothing about others except as a means to the end of ego-aggrandizement.

We can, of course, use art to communicate with ourselves as well as with others. Imagine yourself trapped in a mine by a cave-in, with no hope of rescue before you suffocate or die of thirst. You will never see or speak with another human being again. With plenty of leisure time at your disposal, you might draw a sketch on the mineshaft wall—perhaps a landscape of the world you will never see again. You might draw that sketch as an artist, but you would contemplate it as an audience. And as an audience you might find things in that sketch which, as an artist, you had not intended. The discovery of something new in what you'd drawn would, by definition, be an influence on you. Maybe it would reconcile you to your fate, buried alive deep in the earth, or it might inspire you to redouble your efforts to escape. Or you might notice technical flaws in your sketch, and that might make you try another, an improvement on the first one. And here, of course, art and education have identical motives: to move ourselves and others from ignorance to understanding.

The process of moving others is, obviously, one that requires some degree of co-operation—the audience has to get something out of the experience of art. In several ways, what it gets is analogous to what the artist gains.

The first reward for the audience is a test of self-definition: Is this dance or song or play a way of saying "Me"? Does this expression represent me, speak for me, in some important way? If it does, we respond powerfully and positively, as if we had just gained the power of speech after being kept mute. Alexander Pope called it, "What oft was thought, but ne'er so well expressed." More recent artists and critics call it the shock of recognition.

If the artistic expression does not appear to represent us, we may react apathetically, or even with violent resentment—just as we would if we were forced to utter words that we didn't believe, or had to give an alias instead of our true names. But bear in mind that we may respond as self or as ego. If it's the first, we find something in the artistic expression that defines not only ourselves, but our relations to others. If the work appeals only to the ego in us, it ignores our relationships to others; the rest of the world is only a backdrop for our ego display.

When I talk about nonverbal communication with my students, I sometimes like to dramatize this by taking a handbag from one of my women students and asking a man to walk about the classroom while carrying it. Now, to prove his manhood, a young man will cheerfully carry a football even though possessing it means a risk of serious injury through assault by other young men. Perhaps that's why so many of my male students carry the handbag as if it were a football. Or they adopt exaggerated effeminate mannerisms, to turn the experience into a joke. Quite simply, most young men do not enjoy sending out a "female" message about themselves; most audiences, unless they are very mature and sophisticated and aware of their own shortcomings, don't enjoy art that sends out unpleasant messages about themselves.

The artistic experience is also a suggestion for self-expression: Can I do what the artist is doing? And if I do, can I become what the artist is? Those of us who do become artists generally do so in emulation of some work of art, in response to what it does rather than what it says. We look at the artist's work with a kind of opportunist pragmatism: even if we don't like what the artist is saying or doing, we try to see how we can bend his methods to our own purposes.

For example, very few novels in English deal with the life of the Canadian Inuit, and even fewer from the point of view of the Inuit themselves. But an Inuk could certainly read J.D. Salinger or Margaret Drabble or Mario Vargas Llosa, none of whom has anything at all to say about life in the Arctic. That Inuk could then grasp and exploit the techniques of fiction to his own purposes. I can say that with confidence because it's been done by an Inuk named Markoosie, whose novel *Harpoon of the Hunter* is an exceptionally fine book.

And the artistic experience is also a way for the audience to seek influence or challenge. Is the artist speaking to my interests and concerns as an individual or member of a group? If so, if the artist has shown me something about myself and my people and our circumstances in life, what shall I do as a result? On one level this is the function, of course, of propaganda; George Orwell was right when he said all art is propaganda. He was also right when he said that not all propaganda is art.

Maybe I can clarify the distinction this way: plain propaganda, whether cautious or confident, doesn't really care much about us as persons, as long as we shout the right slogans, vote for the right candidates, buy the right products, and march off to war when required to. It relies on our laziness, our fondness for cliché and stock response, our sentimentality, our ego, and it manipulates us through those weaknesses. Such propaganda is "ego art."

"Self art" may also encourage us to do all these things, but it carries another kind of propaganda message, an unspoken, subliminal message that may even undermine the overt message: *Stay awake! Pay attention! Think! Save your emotions for the people and events that really deserve them! Be honest!*

For many artists, that subliminal propaganda message overwhelms any other. We may listen to Beethoven's *Ode to Joy*, but we can disregard the overt message that all men are brothers, especially if we can't understand German. What impresses us is that an *Ode to Joy* can be conceived, composed, performed, and listened to. As we respond to the message to stay awake, to think, to feel, we also find ourselves eager to pass that message on to others. We may choose this or that overt message as the envelope, but the subliminal message is what we really mean. And this is "self" art.

So art may be propaganda, that is, intended to strengthen some kinds of group values while weakening others. But it's not moral or immoral as such, even when it serves as the vehicle of some moral vision. I think this moral neutrality is one reason for the unpopularity of art among both cautious and confident politicians. It can glorify the state and the status quo, or it can subvert them. It's as neutral as a loaded pistol. Hence the politicians' willingness to suppress any artistic expression they can't control.

"Self" art can be very difficult and demanding for both the audience and the artist. Maybe we don't always feel like staying awake, or we don't like what we notice when we're awake. "Ego" art, by contrast, is usually quite accessible, and the message is more often a lullaby rather than a fire alarm. But don't assume that ego art is always sweet and nice. Melodrama is often violent and upsetting, but its message is usually a lullaby: *The world is just the way you've been taught it is, noisy and gorgeous and stupid, so go back to sleep.* Self art may tell you, without raising its voice, that maybe, just maybe, there's a scorpion in your bed with you.

Now, most people don't like to hear about scorpions in their beds, and the rest of us don't like to hear that Sylvester Stallone's vision of the world is a true one. So self art is unpopular while ego art, which gives the majority what they want, is exceedingly prosperous. That puts artists and their teachers in a difficult position. They have to deal with a widespread public conviction that if the arts are harmless they're trivial entertainment, and if they're not harmless they're subversive.

Sometimes we educators, in defending the arts against such charges, are driven to invoking fuzzy confident-vision arguments about the value of arts education. If only the arts really *did* make us better men and women, wiser human beings, more responsible and compassionate citizens! If they did, of course, those who write biographies of artists would have a much tougher challenge. Fortunately for them, many great artists have been terrible human beings—selfish, vindictive, immature, dishonest, cruel, sexually debauched and perverted, and lacking in table manners. Those of us who study great works of art for a living are not always moral paragons either, or the gossip in faculty dining rooms would be much duller than it is.

So we can't say that either the practice or the study of art is universally "improving" in some socially convenient way. And yet some of us really do stay awake, and think, and feel, as a response to art. Our thoughts and feelings may be disgusting and antisocial, but they are intense and real. That's why education needs the arts, urgently—not for their overt messages, but for just that subversive, unspoken message to stay awake, to think, to feel. And that urgent need puts educators in a wonderfully uncomfortable position.

That's because education functions as the cultural or social equivalent of DNA. It's a way of transmitting information from one generation to the next, retaining useful adaptations and eliminating harmful ones. An organism does this more or less automatically through natural selection; harmful mutations prevent their possessors from reproducing the mutations.

Every culture, from the family unit on up to the world empire, possesses some sense of itself and at least some urge to pass that sense on to its children. That's certainly at the base of the cautious vision and its veneration of the accumulated wisdom of the past. The only exceptions, I suppose, are cultures which are so demoralized that they no longer respect themselves, or confident-vision cultures which are consciously intent on cutting themselves away from a heritage they feel oppressive. China under the Cultural Revolution is a notable example.

Cultures at a certain level of complexity form states, and states pursue their interests in part by education. The state sets up a school system to carry out some kind of social agenda: to assimilate immigrant children, to train people in new technologies, to create access to power for some groups or to deny such access to others. This social agenda, ultimately, is a way of shaping individual and collective identity—a way of enabling people to say, "I am a loyal socialist," or "I am a proud free-enterpriser," "I am Chinese," "I am Canadian." We can't be loyal socialists if we train our children to exploit the workers. Our free-enterprise society is doomed if we teach our children to seek collective solutions to individual problems. So we make some conscious political choices about what we intend to teach, and how we're going to teach it.

Education therefore has, as one of its major functions, the instilling of particular social values that help turn individuals into members of groups. It encourages conformity and collectivity, and wisely so, whether the agenda is confident or cautious.

Now, in many ways education serves the political and administrative needs of the state: We want three thousand aeronautical engineers so we can design a new jetliner that will win us respect, prestige, and foreign exchange. We want four thousand journalists so we can inform our people about what a fine government they have. We want a thousand great athletes so our people will be entertained and distracted from their problems. And we want sixty thousand business managers so our gross national product will go up and we can impose taxes to pay for our new jetliners and our TV networks and our sports stadiums.

That's a pretty straightforward agenda, and most national education systems can meet it. If not, the government can always ship students off to some other country to acquire the training. But the authorities are painfully aware of an insidious problem.

Every time DNA duplicates itself, it risks a copying error that may doom the organism. In education, the analogy might be training a physicist who builds a bomb that blows up the national capital. Or, on the other hand, the copying error in the DNA may lead to a decided advantage for the organism, like a clearer eye or a sharper tooth. In education, the analogy would be a physicist whose training leads to a bomb that blows up someone else's national capital.

Let me shift my metaphors. Every time a new child enters school, we try to copy a body of information and attitudes into that child's head, just as we download a program into a shiny new computer. But even supposedly compatible computers can't always run the same programs. Similarly, every time we accept children into a classroom, we are taking an enormous gamble: Will these kids accept the program and apply it as we wish? Will they garble the program in some unpredictable way? Will the program simply vanish, erased by some internal error, so that the kids are as ignorant as ever?

Or will the kids turn out capable of running the program faster and more effectively than we ever dreamed possible, and find unexpected new uses for it? That possibility, while rare, offers both the hope of an enormous payoff for the state, and the threat of an enormous disaster: *What if the kids want to run things their own way?*

The biologists have a term for a mutant with unknown potential: they call it a "hopeful monster." In education we deal with hopeful monsters all day long, or at least as long as our own hope survives.

If education is a culture's method of reproducing itself and sustaining itself through time, and if cultures must change if they are to survive, then change, the production of hopeful monsters, becomes a worthwhile value to select for. A static, cautious-vision society can content itself with a school system that simply downloads the old program into new computers. Such a society is in a kind of "ego state" instead of in a "self state." An egocentric society sees any change as a threat, something to reject and defend against. A society like ours, however, couldn't stay in an

ego state even if it wanted to. We have to change whether
we like it or not.

So far, I've been discussing education as a function of a
large, powerful, and unified state. But in large enough,
complex enough societies, a kind of tribalistic alienation
sets in. As individuals we have trouble identifying with the
whole society except in times of extreme stress, like a war,
and sometimes not even then. We choose instead to give
our loyalties to a subculture, a tribe.

These tribes have what you might call their "birdsongs,"
ways of announcing their identities and defining their ter-
ritories through cultural expression. Sometimes the birdsongs are actual music—go out and ask the young people
in your neighbourhood if they're rockers, headbangers,
preppies, or some other subculture, and they'll know exactly what you're talking about. (Of course they'll despise
you for trying to categorize them by slang terms doubtless
already out of date.)

Go into any of several urban radio stations in your region and ask why they play golden oldies, pop songs from
the 1950s and '60s. They'll tell you that such music reaches
a commercially interesting group of middle-aged people.

For educators, especially educators in the arts, a problem
arises here. We recognize that in much popular culture,
the anti-culture, we don't hear the self speaking to other
selves, but the ego braying away until some other ego
drowns it out. We don't hear subliminal commands to stay
awake, to think, to feel, but just the reverse: *shut up, shut
down, shut out, shut off*. We recognize that many of the
tribes and subcultures are utterly synthetic, and offer very
little to their members except ruptured eardrums.

But we recognize the validity of the urge to form subcultures, because individuals count for more in small societies than in large ones, and it maddens us when we see
the quest for individuality perverted by the mindless regi-
mentation that so many subcultures impose on their mem-

bers as the price of belonging. And here is one way that
education needs the arts: as a way of helping young people
to form new tribes, new subcultures, that demand wakeful-
ness, thought, and feeling.

When societies change, some groups benefit and others
suffer. Sometimes, for example, a military aristocracy
climbs aboard its horses, draws its sabers, and charges
straight into an artillery barrage. That's the ultimate fate
of any society in a terminal ego state. A new ruling class
rises in its place—the businessmen who built the foundries,
and the engineers who designed the cannons. But the tenure of the new ruling class is insecure. The trick is not
how to make cannons, or how to make bigger cannons, or
how to make nuclear bombs—but how to think about
weapons and warfare in general. Anyone who thinks up
some new weapon, or a new way to neutralize an old one,
can become the agent of revolution.

A society that doesn't want to be overwhelmed by its
neighbours and competitors must therefore try to tackle a
paradox. It needs cautious, loyal conformists who will work
like crazy to protect the status quo, but it also wants them
to be clever, confident mavericks who can come up with
bizarre new ideas, ideas that conformists can't even con-
ceive of. And those ideas will of course threaten the status
quo more effectively than any foreign enemy can, yet the
country's rulers have to be clever mavericks also, to recognize and encourage good ideas when they arise.

This is hard but not impossible. The *daimyo,* the feudal
lords of post-Tokugawa Japan, were just such clever mavericks. After Admiral Perry and his black ships dropped
anchor in Tokyo Bay, the *daimyo* saw they could no longer
hide from the world, and they saw that their own cautious
culture and values would not serve their country well. So
they consciously created a new class of confident western-
ized professionals who could deal on equal terms with the
imperial powers of Europe and America. With less eager-

ness, the octogenarian Communists of China are trying to do something similar today. Both cultures have at least recognized the need for new ideas.

Obviously, those ideas aren't just military ones. A healthy culture needs to constantly re-examine everything it does, from the way it cares for the old to the way it entertains the young. It doesn't need just a loyal opposition, but a kind of "loyal insurgency." The slogan of that insurgency should be: *Stay awake! Think! Feel!*

If education is going to serve the state and the people, it needs to encourage that loyal insurgency—and the arts are a natural hotbed for it. Artists have been bragging for generations about their ability to kick the bourgeoisie in the seat of its collective pants. Well they should, and they should be kicking the aristocrats and the proletarians as well.

I'm not talking about creating scandals in the concert halls and art galleries, though that's a good idea too; I'm not talking about artists going to the barricades to demand bigger state subsidies. I'm not even talking about artists becoming directly involved in politics, though I think that would be a wonderful idea. I am talking about the deliberate encouragement of new ways of perceiving the world, new ways of phrasing the questions of our lives, and I'm talking about disseminating those new perceptions as widely as possible throughout the population.

I am not calling for courses in appreciating rock and roll or comparative graffiti. For most of our young people, the weirdest, most unfamiliar and unsettling art experiences they will ever encounter are the classics; it should only happen more often. I am not looking down my nose at popular culture: It's fine, it's fun, it expresses and defines and moves its audiences.

But because it's so simple, so uniform, it also makes its audiences simple and uniform. Even its wit and irony are self-referential, because it doesn't know anything but itself.

And a culture that knows only itself is in an ego state, not a self state. No matter how rich the exponents of pop culture may become, they and their followers are impoverished and dangerously fragile in a hostile world.

As educators, we are not serving our society well if we allow our students to remain long in an ego state. No matter how passionately our students yearn to attain the intellect of a turnip, we are obliged to goad them back toward consciousness: *Stay awake! Think! Feel!* And not because it's "good for them," but because society won't and can't survive if a majority of us are turnipheads. We must drive our society into a self state, aware of itself and of others, and therefore capable of seeing new solutions to old problems.

Here in British Columbia, our schools have been teaching less art, not more. The problem is that our society is deeply entrenched in an ego state. We have actively discouraged high-school students from studying the fine arts, especially in their last couple of years. They simply can't afford the time and energy, because they won't get into university if they fool around too much with drama or music or painting or creative writing.

A report by the B.C. Arts in Education Council points out that not only are fewer students taking arts courses in the province, but even fewer teachers are available to teach them. In 1992, our secondary schools enrolled just under 228,000 young people. Only seventeen percent of them were enrolled in an art course. Only ten per cent were enrolled in music training. Twelve percent were enrolled in drama. And most of those figures were reductions from the mid-1980s.

The vast majority of our arts enrollments are in the lower grades and therefore, by definition the courses are "kid stuff." By the time students reach Grade 11 and 12, the admissions requirements of post-secondary schools largely determine their course work. Arts courses aren't of much use, so they're squeezed out of a crowded curriculum.

As a result, only eleven percent of our Grade 12 students were enrolled in art in 1992, down from fifteen percent in 1985. Six percent were enrolled in music, down from eight percent in 1985. For drama courses, the enrollment was 4.9 percent, about the same as the mid-'80s figure.

The message here is, of course, that the arts don't really count for much in the hard, cruel world. In fact, the large enrollments in the lower grades suggest that we regard the arts as something like chicken pox—if you expose the kids when they're young, they'll enjoy lifetime immunity.

I am not going to argue that the arts need education only as a source of new recruits. The schools' purpose is not to train office workers and entrepreneurs, and it's not to train painters or choreographers either. *The schools' purpose is to train citizens*, responsible members of society who will put their society in a self state and keep it there, and who will choose their own means of doing so. And that is why education needs the arts, to remind the next generation that they are very much like their parents and grandparents, and very much like their brothers and sisters and cousins around the world.

And why do the arts need education? Despite all those cruel things I said about artists a few moments ago, most artists are already in a high-grade self state, wide awake, thinking, feeling, and all that. They probably glow in the dark, if they're not actually burning with a hard, gemlike flame.

It's been said that the arts can do anything but speak. The aspiring artist may respond very powerfully to a first hearing of the *Ode to Joy*, or a first viewing of *Guernica*. But without knowing something about the traditions that those works come from, and comment upon, the young artist meets my definition of a barbarian: a person ignorant of his own past. Such an artist can respond with energy and talent to the stimuli he encounters, but he's not going to say anything new except by pure chance. He's not even reinventing the wheel; he's reinventing crawling and toddling, and if he's lucky and a genius he may reinvent walking.

It's an agreeable convention in the arts to despise the academy, the dead hand of rules and regulations and unimaginative bureaucracy. For a century or more, being rejected by the academy has been a necessary rite of passage for most of our greatest artists. To be accepted by the academy has been a truly disastrous fate.

Nevertheless, how else are our young artists going to understand what's happening right now unless they check their programs and gain a sense of the context of the present moment? Whatever else our schools may be, they are libraries and museums, repositories of traditions that go back all the way to the Ice Ages. Nowhere else can our young artists gain a systematic understanding of what their art can do, what it has done, what it tries to do, what it might be capable of doing.

William Blake, the 18th-century poet and engraver, once wrote: "I must create my own system or be enslaved by another man's." But he could not have gained even the *idea* of a system without some exposure to education, that is, to systematically organized knowledge and thought.

All too often, the schools live up to their dismal reputation as the academy, the mausoleum of artists who are safely dead and stuffed. That is partly because not enough artists have invaded the academy while they were still alive and kicking to allow their own wild systems to contend with those of the academics. Nevertheless, even at its most stultifying the academy offers the artist not only art but a critical commentary upon art—a voice for art. The young artist may not agree with everything in that commentary, but it is at least a way of testing one's own response against those of others who may not be total blockheads.

If we're not going to produce generation upon generation of barbarian artists in a barbarian society, we should be aggressively teaching the arts and their history. We should also be aggressively teaching the difference between art as anesthetic and art as stimulant. In the process we won't just be running some kind of boot camp for artists; we'll be creating an *audience* for artists, a conscious and literate audience.

I mentioned that artists should be kicking the bourgeoisie, the aristocracy, and the proletariat; those classes should also be capable of kicking back. They should come into studios and recital halls and theatres saying: "I may not know what I like, but I know art."

Imagine the impact on the coterie artist if his coterie expanded into the thousands, the hundreds of thousands. Imagine the challenge to the artist to find that mere shock value can't even shock. What would happen to the avant-garde if its audience was sophisticated enough to know that art may change, but it does not progress? Andy Warhol is not 25,000 years better than the cave painters of Lascaux— only 25,000 years different. If art doesn't progress, then of course it has no vanguard—only artists trying their best to do something with whatever they have at hand, which is now a tradition, in virtually every art, extending back thousands of years.

You may be reflecting that the bourgeoisie, the aristocracy, and the proletariat are already quite capable of kicking artists without being provoked into doing so. But it's an uninformed philistinism; society should be kicking its artists because it cares about art.

The arts need education also as an ally in the endless battle with the Philistines. Here in B.C., arts educators have found themselves arguing for support on the grounds that their graduates will become immensely rich, or if that's too hard to swallow, arts graduates will at least provide a lot of tax revenue and spinoff jobs, etc. etc. That's what happens when the Philistines set the terms of debate. Remember that I said the function of the schools is to produce citizens, not workers. Well-educated citizens know perfectly well that they need to work. They also know that *the arts are work*, whether they bring in millions or not a penny.

The arts need education, then, not to create more artists—artists usually select themselves—but to create a culture in which the arts can flourish. If they remain the concern only of a coterie, even if that coterie is a sizable fraction of one of the more prosperous social classes, the arts are finished. In effect, they put themselves in that mine shaft, on the wrong side of the cave-in; they may amuse themselves painting pretty pictures on the rock face for a while, but eventually the air and light will go. The arts may indulge themselves in contempt for the groundlings who will never see or appreciate those lovely sketches on the rock face, but that's not much consolation.

Education needs the arts, in part, to produce mavericks who look at the world from unexpected angles, who generate hitherto unthinkable ideas, because otherwise the state is doomed to sink into an ego state and eventually die. The arts need education for precisely the same reason: to equip young artists with an array of information that will enable them to extend the boundaries of their art. Otherwise art itself will sink into an ego state.

Within science fiction, my own field, there is a branch of stories about space-flight. In these stories, we suppose that we will never exceed the speed of light, or come anywhere near it, yet we will nevertheless try to reach other solar systems at enormous distances from this planet. So we decide to build what is sometimes called a "generation ship." This is a spacecraft so big that it's sometimes hollowed out of an asteroid, or built as a rotating cylinder fifty or sixty kilometers long and twenty kilometers across—big enough so that crops can be grown, animals can be raised, and families can flourish for centuries while the ship slowly creeps across interstellar space.

The trouble with this idea is that such a miniature ecosystem would surely fail long before its inhabitants reached another star. Big as it might seem to its crew—especially those who were born in the ship and who had never known earth—it would be a tiny, frail and vulnerable bubble of life in a hostile emptiness. Its systems would be complex enough to guarantee an eventual failure, but not complex enough to survive such a failure. These miniature worlds might survive close to the sun, but not out in the dark and the cold.

In the same way, the arts can't seal themselves off and hope for some eventual safe arrival at a welcoming new world. It is this world or none; nothing simpler than the whole world can support us.

A culture in an ego state is aware of outside influences only as threats, and it tries to ward off those threats one way or another. Those threats are real. When the Soviet bloc let down its barriers against the outside world, its member states changed overnight under the new western influences. If a nation like Canada let down its barriers, so the argument goes, we would soon be just another faceless suburb of American culture.

But a fully mature self art ceases to regard other cultures as "other"—they are simply aspects of a single vast and complex human culture, from which its members can take whatever they like to express what they think and feel and perceive, the way Markoosie took the European art form of the novel and bent it to his own purposes.

We can't close our borders against the invasion of popular or foreign culture; offense is our best defence, and we should be invading *their* terrain, appropriating every good thing we run across. We can't do that unless we have two things: hundreds of thousands of troops recruited in school theatres and studios and music rooms, and the confidence that our cause is just and our arts as good as any in the world.

Those might seem like impossible stipulations, especially after the depressing figures about the state of arts education here in B.C. But scores of thousands of us have given our short lives to the fostering of the arts in the classroom and the marketplace; if we don't believe our cause is just and our arts are worthwhile, we're in the wrong business altogether. As for the troops—just step into your local school and take a look. There they are, busy making the whole world's arts their own property.

And the Rest of the Curriculum?
What I've said about teaching the arts applies equally, I think, to the other traditional subjects. Each is a long dialogue with the world. Physicists take part in one dialogue, geographers in another, historians in a third. We started listening not long ago, and our students have just walked in. If they're going to make sense of what they hear, our job as teachers is to provide a summary of what's gone on so far: "Galileo's right but politically incorrect. Newton's right except at the quantum level, and for that you have to talk to Bohr and Heisenberg and Einstein."

Again the issue is to find a balance among training, schooling, and education. In physics, the student needs training in the scientific method of empirical observation and logical deduction; schooling in the body of theoretical and practical knowledge acquired through Newton, Faraday, and their followers; education in acquiring the attitude of scientific inquiry within this and other fields.

For a tiny minority of students, physics in high school is the introduction to a career as a working scientist. But that doesn't mean the rest of the class is exempt from serious, rigorous study of the subject. Half a century ago, a few physicists put their subject on the curriculum with a vengeance by building the first atomic bombs. The citizen-proprietors of modern democracies therefore have an obligation to understand physics well enough to frame and enforce wise policy on the building and use of nuclear weapons.

So, just as students of the arts need to know the history of art before they can understand what their artist-classmates are doing, student citizens need to understand the basic principles of science, the broad outline of recent and ancient history, and other fields that throw light on present and future policies. Otherwise, when their turn comes to take charge, they will only repeat the mistakes of the past. That is what barbarians do.

I am not arguing that students should know all these disciplines only as a background to helping to shape informed policy. The more they know, the more knowledge they can apply to other knowledge and the more surprising connections they can make. That is what intelligent people do. But students should certainly not acquire knowledge of all these subjects merely as a convenience to their future teachers in the universities. The post-secondary professoriat, like students, believes in the conservation of intellectual energy. Faculty don't want to teach simple, boring stuff; they want to get straight to wherever the frontier is in their discipline, and they see their students' function as doing the campsite chores. Hence all the faculty complaints about the dreadful job the schools are doing in preparing students to be underpaid flunkies of well-paid professors. That the students might have their own agenda is a thought that rarely crosses a professor's mind.

In the scholarly or critical approach to the arts, we also need to know what has gone before and where the dialogue is leading. Here we feel less secure, however. Arts scholarship has always been a genteel occupation, a kind of hobby for a handful of aristocrats which we have now made a mandatory part of every child's education. Historically, reading literature was a highly specialized form of entertainment; the idea of studying it systematically would have seemed bizarre to all but the most protected and affluent connoisseurs.

The success of the education bureaucracy has encouraged us to forget that, less than a century ago, English literature (among other modern disciplines) was not an academic subject. Everyone expected an educated person to keep up with current writing as a matter of course, and to assess it in the light of the classic authors of the past. One might, as a fan, learn a great deal about Swinburne or Bret Harte, but the idea of teaching such authors in school would have seemed as strange as teaching a contemporary course in Gene Roddenberry as creator of *Star Trek* or the poetic theory underlying Michael Jackson's songs. (If Roddenberry and Jackson don't seem all that strange, it's because we now have too many graduate students and not enough serious topics for their dissertations.)

However, now that they can earn a good living by imitating the literary hobbies of ancient dilettantes, some scholars and their apprentices are looking for more congenial ways to spend their time. And that takes us into the embarrassing topic of The Canon.

The Canon and the Corruption of Literary Studies

Teaching jobs pay pretty well and offer good security if you can survive seniority-driven layoffs in your early career. Those simple facts make education an attractive career to many people in ethnic, racial, and cultural minorities. In addition, pursuit of more education is beginning to pay off in other career fields once closed to minorities and women. But some members of such groups, inspired by the confident vision, have acquired an attitude of contempt toward the culture of education as they see it: a culture that is white, patriarchal, and oppressive to all but a favored few. (Few reflect that white male educators, themselves imbued with the confident vision, promoted the idea of sexual and racial equality in the first place, and saw improved access to education as the best means to achieve it.)

This has led to problems in curriculum in the public schools and post-secondary alike. I can't speak with much authority about the impact in most disciplines, but in the teaching of literature the problem of the canon is real. After hearing about strange debates in American universities, about the canon and dead white males and Eurocentric education, we now see the debate has moved into our own high schools.

The debate is anything but academic. Its outcome will decide what we teach in English courses for the next decade or two. It will help to shape Canadian society, defining what is worth studying and why. As in many other cases, we are trying to deal as Canadians with an American controversy that affects us only indirectly. But affect us it does, and we had better think it through before it completely takes over the terms of debate.

American opponents of the traditional English curriculum offer something like the following argument:

1. The canon of traditional English literature (as well as history, political science, the arts, and other subjects) simply reflects the political power of a vanished generation. Anglo-Saxon males dominated the English-speaking world for centuries, and imposed their values on women and on the nations they conquered. The literature of these dead white males has no particular merit in itself. If live white males are still in power, they shouldn't be.

2. Subjugated groups—women, blacks, Asians, Native Indians and others—have their own social values and their own artistic expressions of them. These expressions are just

as good as those of the white male canon. Indeed, they may be even better, morally and esthetically, since they deal with experiences beyond the range and interest of dead white males.

3. To teach the white male canon, while neglecting other works of literature, is especially narrow-minded when our classes are full of women and minority groups. This neglect tells such students that they are not as important or deserving of study as dead white males. A Eurocentric curriculum diminishes members of other cultures.

4. English teachers therefore should adopt a multicultural curriculum that exposes students to a much wider range of literature, art, and social values. Otherwise we will simply perpetuate the oppression of a bygone era.

When the president of the B.C. English Teachers' Association, Steve Naylor, raised this issue in his association newsletter, he made his own divided feelings clear. He loves the traditional body of English literature, but he also respects the views of minority advocates. Indeed, he quotes extensively from American multiculturalists. I share Naylor's divided feelings, but I think the confident-vision multicultural approach actually aggravates the racism and sexism it wants to remedy. It even threatens the literature of the oppressed groups that it purports to champion.

Northrop Frye argued that value judgments indeed have no place in literary criticism. Shakespeare is not better than Marlowe, not even better than the writers of *Married . . . with Children*. To prefer Shakespeare is a matter of taste, not of objective merit. Nevertheless, we do tend to teach more Shakespeare than Marlowe, and very few high school English teachers would see much use in classroom study of last week's *Married . . . with Children*.

Is this simply the Eurocentric male bias of the curriculum? Naylor approvingly quotes the black American educator Charles Johnson's argument that, "It would be unwise for our students to read only the works of 'dead white male authors'— We should balance them with works by authors of other cultures and ethnic backgrounds."

Should we then balance *Othello* by giving equal time to James Baldwin or NWA? If we teach "To His Coy Mistress," should we balance it with selections from Andrea Dworkin? Or is "balance" itself a misleading word? Balance is what we seek when we hear a debate. We want a full, fair argument from every side, so that we can then judge which argument seems most sound in the light of all possible information.

But we do not teach geometry by balancing the axioms of that dead white male Euclid against the mathematics of the Mayas. We do not teach history by balancing the First World War against the Chaco War fought between Paraguay and Bolivia in the 1930s. No one since Hitler has suggested that modern physics is a Jewish science; no one says some neglected Palestinian physicist ought to get equal time with Einstein in Physics 12.

Quite simply, Shakespeare has had more historical impact than Marlowe, influencing far more subsequent writers and readers. Maya mathematicians in their time were more advanced than those of Europe and Asia, but their mathematics vanished in the Spanish Conquest.

We may, if we wish, regret such historical events, but we have trouble denying them. Frye defines a classic as a book that refuses to go away. So when a cultural force like Shakespeare refuses to go away, only a Maoist-style book-burning cultural revolution has much chance of suppressing his influence.

Balance presents another hazard. If we are to regard the curriculum as a kind of debate among contending values, the implication is that the students, as judges, will then decide in someone's favor and reject everyone else. Literature, art, and other social values then become simply consumer items, like shampoo or designer jeans—not just a matter of personal taste but a fashion statement. Worse yet, the arts become tribal totems, like the pop music groups who define their audiences. Far from broadening their audiences' tastes, such groups only encourage mutual contempt and stereotyping.

We should study the successes of English literature because they are successes, because they influenced *other* successes, not because they glorify armored thugs like Beowulf or indecisive princes like Hamlet.

Nor should we study them because their authors were male. Naylor expresses relief that in B.C. intermediate-grade reading lists, gender equity prevails: half the novels are by women. It's not clear whether those novels got on the list through their literary qualities or the sex of their authors. I hope it was through their qualities; I cannot imagine a more patronizingly sexist attitude than to study an author's work because of her gender and not her ability.

"Equity" also condemns non-white authors to a permanent ghetto. We must read Chinua Achebe because he is *black*, not because he is good. Salman Rushdie becomes merely a Third World author unpopular in Islamic countries. And what are we to make of Kazuo Ishiguro, a thoroughly British novelist? Do we approve of him as a genetically acceptable Asian, or reject him because he chronicles the lives of Anglo-Saxon males?

In effect, we are doing what Northrop Frye long ago warned us against: judging literature by non-literary yardsticks, and degrading it in the process. We are saying that literature is of little importance in itself, except as an expression of political and social values: the supremacy of the English aristocracy, or the merit of the working classes, or the innate goodness of Peruvian peasant women. In other words, the literature we should teach is merely the propaganda of whoever happens to be in power at the moment—or wants to be.

So if, say, Asian women were to rule Canada, we would

all have to teach Joy Kogawa and Evelyn Lau and Sky Lee. As soon as this dictatorship fell at the hands of freedom-loving men of Icelandic descent, we'd all have to junk our curriculum whether those authors were any good or not, and start teaching the Icelandic sagas and W.D. Valgardson.

Worse yet, advocates of these non-literary yardsticks guard their own cultures jealously. The Writers' Union of Canada, and now the Canada Council, have been tying themselves in knots over whether authors have the right to portray characters not of their own race or culture. If they don't, then a white woman of Scots descent dare not write about the experience of a Native Indian woman. A black Jamaican man has no business exploring the emotions of a Ukrainian-Canadian man. And while cross-dressing might be politically acceptable, daring to portray someone of the opposite sex in a literary work is out of the question.

I'm not talking about doing such things well or badly; I'm talking about doing them *at all.* This position means that no author is really free to write anything except autobiography. I can write only about being a white male college teacher living in the Vancouver suburbs. My student from Mount Currie cannot write about anything beyond the boundaries of her reserve. Neither of us better say anything critical of any other identifiable group except white males.

Now, it may well be that many writers cannot make an honest, perceptive imaginative leap into the mind and experience of different people; if they try and fail, we can certainly criticize them for their failure. But to suppose we can forbid them from even *trying* is not only arrogant, it says the whole purpose of communication through literature is beside the point.

If you cannot accurately portray a person different from yourself, you presumably can't understand that person's experience in the first place. It is so alien to your own that you really have nothing in common. Even experiences like walking down the street or doing a job are utterly different because of race or sex. You might as well write nothing; only clones of yourself will know what you're talking about.

So black women should quit writing even about their own experience; white and Asian women just won't get it any more than men will. Literature itself is pointless; its whole premise is that people can indeed understand one another if only they share a language and the works written in it. Instead of transcending racial and sexual differences through literature, we must now admit that race and sex are the only things that really matter about any individual—that racism and sexism should dominate our dealings with one another.

The idea of a balanced multicultural curriculum encourages a particularly fatuous kind of racism. Forgetting the incommunicability of being a Native Indian woman or a Chinese-Canadian man, the balance argument holds that reading something by another Native Indian or another Chinese-Canadian is good for the minority student's self-esteem. Again this fosters an empty tribalism, as if one shared the glory of publication with a Native Indian or Chinese-Canadian author.

This approach is more concerned with socializing students than with training their intellects. We might as well include works written by hemophiliacs, or left-handers, or amputees—all of them no older than our students, of course, or we risk oppressing them with our ageist bias.

Multiculturalists might argue that such writers provide role models, and that their subjects affirm the validity of minority readers' experience. But by that argument Homer is an inspiration only to Bronze Age Greeks and Ralph Ellison an inspiration only to black male New Yorkers now in extreme old age. (The columnist Robert Fulford once observed that Shakespeare as a white male role model can only fill white male students with despair at ever approaching his level of skill.) We can't have it both ways: We can't say dead white males offer nothing for minorities, while minorities mysteriously offer so much to one another.

Well, am I arguing that we trot right through the Anglo-Saxon male canon from Beowulf to D.H. Lawrence, with just a gentlemanly tip of the hat to the Brontës and George Eliot? Not at all. But we cannot understand the varieties of literature—even those in our particular language—until we understand their sources. Every literary work is, among other things, a comment on everything the author has read before. That's why Northrop Frye suggested that close enough study of any work of literature would eventually lead us into a study of *all* literature.

So we can't fully understand the work of Joy Kogawa until we place it in a context of English, Canadian, American, and Japanese literature. We can't fully appreciate James Baldwin until we know the Bible that inspired his own education. And when we come to look at literary works outside the mainstream of English literature, they will mean very little to us unless we have something to compare them with.

Culture is no one's property, and everyone's. I can take no credit for Bach and Goethe just because some of my ancestors were Germans. Bryan Adams is a North Vancouver boy as well as a Canadian, but that doesn't vindicate my own nationality or choice of residence.

But Bach and Goethe and Bryan Adams all belong to me, say something to me, say something about me. I don't understand Montagnais, but the Native Indian pop group Kashtin is part of my culture. My family includes the author of Ecclesiastes, Charles Dickens, Gabriel Garcia Marquez, and Margaret Atwood. It also includes my relative the Lady Murasaki, who wrote *The Tale of Genji* about the time that Leif Eiriksson (another relative) was sailing to Newfoundland. I would no sooner reject a new relative from a foreign culture than I would reject a large sum of Swiss francs or Japanese yen—or a Bill Reid carving.

As an English teacher in China, I needed to explain every passing reference and expression in even the simplest short story by Hemingway or the briefest poem by Robert Frost. The cultural matrix just wasn't there. But one morning as I was explaining Archibald MacLeish's *Ars Poetica*, a Chinese teaching colleague raised his hand. He came from an academic family, and during the Cultural Revolution, his parents had taught him English even though an interest in foreign languages and literature could get you in terrible trouble in those days. After all, western culture was decadent, and carried "spiritual pollution." Nevertheless he had risked everything to master the literature of dead white imperialist males. Now he raised his hand and pointed out that the images in MacLeish's poem, when he sight-translated them back into Chinese, were deeply familiar ones from Chinese poetry of a millennium ago.

Would you be surprised if I told you that was one of the greatest moments I have experienced in over twenty-five years of teaching? Would you be surprised if I told you that student is now a professor of English literature at a great university in the United States? And can you imagine how impoverished we both would have been, had we stayed within the boundaries some people would have liked to impose on us?

By all means, let us teach works by women, by people from varied ethnic and racial backgrounds, by people whose sexuality has developed in many different ways. But let us not demean either the works or their authors by making them *no more* than women, *no more* than racial or ethnic representatives, *no more* than sexual beings. If they are worth our attention, it is as writers with something worth saying about the human condition that we all share. They deserve judgment by the same standards we use to judge the authors of the past. If they meet those standards, their books will refuse to go away and they will in turn influence other writers.

But we cannot judge them properly—in fact all we can do is patronize and insult them—if we do not have a context for them. That context is the literature to which they are now contributing, the literature of dead white males that we English teachers should be proud to teach.

6

A 21st-Century Curriculum

Imagine that you work for a big company. Your workspace is less than one square metre, and your chair is hard. Normally you can't even leave it without your supervisor's permission. You have no privacy. Although you can't even talk to your fellow-workers without permission, the noise level is high. Your workplace is aggressively ugly. Corridors, like working areas, are drab and bare. Supervisors take their breaks in comfortable lounge areas. You must settle for a noisy, echoing cafeteria or the corridors.

You have to work for several different supervisors, all of whom consider their own assignments the most urgent. They rarely co-ordinate their assignments so you can tackle them systematically. The assignments often seem meaningless to you, and don't always make sense to the supervisors either. Their explanations, sometimes given with great sarcasm, are bafflegab.

But the work's not important. It's always being interrupted by administrative announcements and by company events supposedly intended to raise your morale. Plenty of your fellow-workers get promoted even though everyone knows their work's no good. If your work is good, you will get a reputation as a brown-noser.

While you must put up with countless petty rules, you're not always safe at work. Supervisors seem unable to stop sexual harassment, theft, drug abuse, racist and sexist insults, and outright physical assault—all committed by employees on company property. Some employees carry weapons because they consider themselves in danger whenever they're in the workplace.

You have no say in working conditions, and the Charter of Rights doesn't seem to apply to you. Exercising your freedom of speech could get you suspended or even fired. You have freedom of assembly only on your supervisors' terms. They routinely exchange confidential information about you, and may casually slander you in the process. Given these conditions, it's not surprising that ten to forty percent of your fellow-workers quit every year, even if their only alternatives are a dead-end job or unemployment. Supervisors don't seem to care much about the attrition rate.

No, you wouldn't want to work for this company. In fact, you might want to take it to court. But for too many of our children, high school is just such a company.

Granted, puberty makes it hard for many young people to work effectively without strong supervision. But the present high-school atmosphere too often combines intellectual slackness and bureaucratic tyranny. It serves neither students nor their future employer—nor their teachers, when you think about it.

Instead, high schools actually encourage a convict-like, anti-intellectual, us-against-them teen anti-culture among many students. They fight the system just to preserve a shred of self-respect. They develop a passive-aggressive attitude, expressed in slovenly work, insolence, contempt for intellect, and vandalism.

Too harsh a picture? Remember those success rates, and give me a better reason for them. Right now, in any given class of B.C. Grade 8 students, *one in three* won't graduate from Grade 12 on schedule—if ever. If you believe in the cautious vision, you may not care about that failure and noncompletion rate; it just means a tough process is in place and not all can survive it. But you'd better explain how you propose to cope in a society filling up fast with unemployable young people. If you believe in the confident vision, you may be ready to junk traditional standards and subjects as a price you're glad to pay if it helps more kids graduate. But you'd better explain how you propose to cope in a society filling up fast with equally unemployable young people whose graduation certificates mean nothing.

Improving our students' success rates—and ensuring that their successes are real—will demand changes in everything from school architecture to the attitudes of teachers and parents. Perhaps the most important change would be to consider secondary education as the deadly serious, life-or-death business that it is. Without such change, we'll go on losing a third of our future brainpower—the kids who are at least smart enough to see that today's schools are not for them.

When I first presented this portrait of high school in the late 1980s, the then education minister, Tony Brummet, dropped me a note about my "satirical" approach. I didn't, and don't, see anything satirical about it at all. Even Albert Shanker, the head of the American Federation of Teachers, has called the public schools the last "command economy" on the Soviet model. Just as the Soviets created the very worker alienation that Marx condemned as a curse of capitalism, bureaucratic education fosters the ignorance and intellectual stagnation of the people it says it's serving.

If anything, matters are worse now than they were five years ago. The bureaucratic structure is itself a kind of curriculum, steering students and teachers alike in certain directions and blocking them if they try to go elsewhere. The structure carries a powerful nonverbal message (and we always trust the nonverbal message, especially when it contradicts the verbal one): learning comes in minutes and hours, not in insights and concepts. Administrative needs always take priority over learning. The only kind of knowledge worth having is what a teacher can quantify. The demands of next year's course (or of post-secondary education, years away) determine what you should learn this year. Democracy is a charade, with student involvement limited to planning social events. Success—or at least the pleasure of being left alone—depends on remaining in a state of infantile dependence on one's teachers and administrators. Whether you're cautious or confident, you should regard this status quo as unacceptable.

We can't carry on as we have. If we do, the result will be similar to the education system I saw in Mexico forty years ago. That system offered good schools to the few who could afford them, and dreadful schools to the vast majority. It is a tempting system, especially to cautious middle-class parents who want to protect their children from poverty and to smooth the path to secure jobs in business and the professions. If we adopt such a system we will consign ourselves to the Third World.

But suppose we choose instead to see education with stereoscopic vision, to see it as a process that enables students both to maximize their own freedom of choice (a cautious-vision ideal) and to recognize that their freedom is contingent on that of their fellow-citizens (a confident-vision ideal).

Suppose we wanted to encourage an information-based economy, and we recognized that small entrepreneurial employers create far more jobs than do big corporations. Suppose further that we explicitly declared the function of education to be the training of *citizens*, not of workers and consumers. And finally suppose that we wished to encourage an environmentally sustainable society that places little value on growth and consumption for their own sake.

We realize that very few people can afford to pay the

whole cost of a child's education. Nor can society afford to pay the cost of neglecting that education. That's why we tax ourselves and subsidize parents and children. And we elect some of our fellow-citizens to oversee the process so that we get results desirable to a majority of taxpayers. School is a public enterprise, just like building roads and bridges, which means it should be most concerned with public benefits—not just private advantages. If we keep that in mind, much of the curriculum will develop logically and naturally.

Historically, most children have experienced school as a succession of failures and humiliations; we should offer them a series of successes. This is not a matter of building empty "self-esteem" at the price of real achievement, but of showing children that learning is a strategy for making sense of their chaotic world. Nor is it a matter of shielding them from failure. Failure is dangerous only when children see it as an outcome of learning, not as an outcome of ignorance. School should therefore produce graduates whose confidence borders on cheerful arrogance. But they should also be responsible citizens with a proprietor's concern about their society.

If we accept those premises, and understand the multicultural society we are developing in Canada, then we can describe the rough outlines of a school system that can help produce the kind of people Canadians should be in the next century.

• *The system is increasingly diverse, offering curriculums for many different cultures, classes and lifestyles.* "Streaming" was an attempt to do so, but produced only a kind of typecasting. But once the system gives up the confident delusion of "equal" education for all, genuine education for all becomes possible. It means a Native Indian can go to school in her own language, immerse herself in her own culture, and still play a part of her own choosing in the larger society. It means a learning-disabled child can grow around his disabilities, identify and develop his skills, and go into the larger society with something to contribute.

Breaking up the system into airtight, mutually hostile ghettoes is no answer at all. No school should prepare its students only for life in some kind of ethnic theme park or sheltered workshop. Instead, a truly diverse curriculum should equip its students to gain reasonable access to all parts of the larger society without compromising the identity they have gained from their own communities. Done right, diverse schools respect students' individual backgrounds while weakening their tendency to tribalism.

• *The system fosters independent learning and critical thinking at all levels.* It has to; it doesn't have enough good teachers to survive in classical full-frontal supervisory mode. Twenty-first-century teachers are instigators, provocateurs, librarians, and mentors. As teachers of critical thinking they are prepared to take some hard punches aimed at them and the schools—and to punch back as friendly but serious sparring partners. Teachers want students to "own" what they learn, not just rent it until the next exam. That means they're prepared to let students take off in their own direction, not just follow the teacher's plan.

The demand for critical thinking also means a respectful but relentless questioning of stereotypes, conventional wisdom, and orthodoxy. The kid who says "Girls are no good at math," should be prepared to defend her assertion or abandon it. The teacher who says "Spelling is important," had better present cogent reasons; teachers who can't do so have no business in the classroom.

One of the most offensive depictions of teaching in modern cinema occurs in the film *Stand and Deliver*, in which a Chicano math teacher urges his Hispanic/Indian students to master calculus by asserting: "You have the blood of mathematicians in your veins." Such an appeal to racism ought to be part of every school's curriculum—as an example of how *not* to think critically and independently. But strong reasoning skills should lead more students into mathematics and the sciences, and to experience greater success in those fields.

• *The system is interested in standards, but not in standardization.* It would like all graduates to know the details of the Riel Rebellion and basic trigonometry, but it doesn't much care how or when students learn them. It counts on teachers' competence to help instil knowledge, and it expects teachers to assess learning without leaning on multiple-choice exams or other illusions of quantifiable measurement. (Yes, exams for aspiring surgeons and airline pilots are at least as rigorous as in the 1990s. But the old test-givers may be out of a job, as we'll see when we look at post-secondary problems.)

In many cases the exams do not test knowledge in memory but the ability to define a problem and then find and make sense of relevant knowledge in books, periodicals, online databases, and other resources—which is what we do outside school.

• *By welcoming older people back into school, the system helps teach everyone about others' needs and abilities.* Adults with inadequate skills are as unacceptable as unskilled teenagers. We should be making a return to school a requirement of anyone lacking literacy or numeracy, whatever their age. Young people gain a sense of continuity with the past; older people face the challenges of new ideas and values. In many subjects (notably computers and other technical fields), age is unimportant. A middle-aged man can learn from a thirteen-year-old girl and vice versa. Age mixing will occur more on the post-secondary level, but it may well occur in the public schools as well.

• *The system is training citizens, not employees.* However, a good citizen ought to do all right whether as a worker or as an employer. Having succeeded in working both independently and in small co-operative groups, graduates are ready to strike out on their own when they enter the working world. They tend to reject "organization man" careers; in fact, they tend to reject the very idea of a lifetime career. They prefer to master a set of skills, use them for a time, and move on to a new challenge—perhaps after a brief return to school. But they do work well on the job, especially when it demands constant innovation and offbeat thinking. They shun routine, repetitive work as worse than a waste of time.

• *The system enables students to gain access to information.* Knowing how to get the facts enables students and graduates to judge the value of various political issues—to decide, for example, whether logging another valley or accepting another group of refugees is in everyone's best interests. They can also tell when they lack enough information, and they know where to find it. They debate a lot, they recognize manipulation when they see it, and they suspect those who try to manipulate them.

If their education disposes them to independent thinking and skeptical inquiry, it also tries to guard against the vices of those virtues: prejudging most information as garbage and making snap decisions based on too little good information. If the children of the 1980s and '90s think ill of themselves, the tendency of early 21st-century children is to arrogance, contempt for ignorance whatever its cause, and even complacency about their own abilities.

The education system I propose is, in one sense, highly subversive. It is *not* trying to sustain a particular culture or ideology, cautious or confident. It is *not* a method for projecting adult anxieties onto children—to make them "competitive," for example, because we currently see Japan and Germany as somehow outdoing us. It is not an elaborate way to say: "Do as I tell you." Schools for chaos want only to create free citizens who can make their own intelligent, informed decisions about what to do with their lives. Let's remember that a liberal education is one that prepares young people for *libertas*—for freedom. And they need it because freedom is not something we're born with but something we learn.

We learn it in large part by gaining useful workplace skills. Without them we are the slaves of our bellies and anyone who will give us work for food. If we have practical skills, we have what some people call "drop-dead money": when someone demands something of us that we don't choose to give, we can say, "Drop dead," and walk away to a better offer.

We can hope that free citizens value their freedom and civic responsibilities as much as (or more than) we ourselves do. But we cannot force them to be free, or compel them to be responsible. We cannot threaten them into admiring Shakespeare or Montaigne, Emily Carr or Margaret Atwood. Nor can we brainwash them into political correctness and environmental conservation. But if we show them that life is deeper, broader, richer, and funnier thanks to education for freedom, they should be wise enough to pass the lesson on to their children.

Well, this all sounds noble and uplifting, but what would they actually *know* as a result of such an education? In a sense, it doesn't matter; we are not just training students for the current workplace, and we are not training them just for the next bureaucratic box. But we do want to give them some useful knowledge that they can connect to other knowledge, and we very much want them to maintain the toddler's attitude that learning is a good thing to do both for the immediate pleasure it gives and for the increased power it grants the learner. Remember that a good education equips you to know how to learn fast in response to the unpredictable.

But given what I understand about the nature of the chaotic world of the next century, I could suggest that our children should reach age eighteen in the early 21st century with demonstrated competence in the following subjects:

- *Fluency in English and French*, and at least a reading knowledge of a third language. By fluency I mean the ability to speak and write correctly, to listen and read with comprehension on at least the level of a Grade 6 or 7 student of the other language group. The third language might be anything from Cree to Cantonese, but Spanish would likely be the most useful. Much of the Pacific Rim, after all, is Hispanic; that includes a large part of the western United States.

- *The Bible as a literary, historical and cultural document*, as well as other basic documents of Christianity, Judaism, Islam, Hinduism, Sikhism, Buddhism, and Native Indian religions. Our failure to use the Bible in school has made much literature, music, and art incomprehensible to young people. As a result, children of narrow-minded fundamentalists are more culturally literate than their secular contemporaries. Equally objectionable is the grubby bigotry that thrives on ignorance of other people's religious beliefs and values. At least one course in comparative religions ought to be mandatory before Grade 10.

- *The physical and biological sciences.* If we could put people on the moon, a quarter-century later we should be able to explain how we did it. The chemistry of ozone loss, the disappearance of the Atlantic cod fishery, and a host of other issues require a scientifically literate population. We should be teaching applied sciences, not just academic disciplines whose only purpose is to prepare students for the next level of abstraction. A certain amount of theory is helpful, but emphasis should fall on the principles we use in our technology. Students who understand those principles are ready for both advanced study and apprenticeship in the technical workplace.

- *Mathematics at least to calculus.* This will probably mean starting earlier and working faster in math than we've been accustomed to. Any number of countries, from Singapore to Hungary, show it's possible. But again the math should be practical. Otherwise it's an empty exercise for all but a handful of students.

- *Philosophy from Plato to Marx*, with emphasis on ethics and logic. Apart from useful training in critical thinking, the history of philosophy would throw light on a great deal of history that otherwise looks like demented melodrama: the French revolution, the rise and fall of Soviet communism, the coexistence of slavery and democracy in the United States.

- *Basic economic theory from Adam Smith to Milton Friedman*. If nothing else, such training would tend to immunize young people against the cautious and confident orthodoxies of the day. Understanding the economic philosophy underlying different nations' policies—Germany, Japan, Singapore, Mexico—would equip them to compete more intelligently, if competition is necessary.

- *Canadian and world history*. No society can function long in an amnesic condition, and it shouldn't have to re-invent the proverbial wheel either. The study of history would show students that nations may rise and fall, but cultures can last for thousands of years—as ancient Roman culture still flourishes in Mediterranean and Latin American countries.

- *English and North American literature* with some exposure to European, Latin American, and Asian literatures, and at least one ancient literature. Students ought to know at least two or three of the major Chinese poets as well as they know the English Romantics, and should have some familiarity with the literature of ancient Greece, Rome, or India.

- *Public speaking* (and listening). To our shame, we live in a nation that guarantees us freedom of speech, where everyone is terrified of speaking to any group larger than three. Most educated adults wince at the painful inarticulacy of many young people; such children are trapped in a limited dialect because they have no practice in speaking anything else. No one should leave school without the repeated experience of addressing at least one hundred listeners. A quiet classrom is the devil's playground. Everyone should speak daily in class, to the class, for at least three consecutive minutes. If the speech is a matter of reading aloud, then reading skills will also improve.

- *Physical education.* We will pay a high price for the last decade's neglect of this discipline. Every student should learn how to achieve maximum physical grace, strength, and co-ordination. We have deluded ourselves that phys. ed. is just a process for selecting naturally talented athletes, and that we can afford to sacrifice it in hard times.

- *The history of western art since the Greeks,* and some knowledge of non-European traditions. The history of western music since the middle ages. At least two years of a performing art, whether music, dance or drama. Not to include these elements would be to rob young people of an enormous heritage.

- *Frequent experience in writing for a large audience,* whether by producing a class newspaper or magazine every year, or by writing letters, briefs, and proposals to editors, politicians, and the community. The present emphasis on academic essay writing promotes a rarefied and advanced skill, better suited to educated adults than to children. Trying to develop the skill in children is to train them only in sterile formula: thesis paragraph, three paragraphs of "development," and closing paragraph. Worse yet, the only reader is a harassed teacher trying to get through a stack of thirty essays at a time.

With writing skills, reading follows more readily. My own experience as a teacher of writing has shown me that this is the most powerful means available for young people to take a part in the larger community. Every spray-painted graffito reflects that understanding, but real mastery of writing for a public is a form of power every student should possess.

• *Comfortable use of computer technology* not only as a tool for writing but also as a means of communication and research. I will have more to say on this subject later; the computer will become a kind of school in itself.

Now, you could no doubt think of more subjects, but I'm dealing here with a no-frills core curriculum.

I know it all sounds impossibly weird and Utopian. But given the kind of chaotic future I've described—multicultural, economically turbulent, demographically skewed—what would you remove from that curriculum, and how would you propose to deal with the social consequences of its removal? If we teach our students only one thing, it should be that H.G. Wells was right—we are in a race between education and catastrophe, and we're coming into the home stretch.

Should we teach all these subjects in separate courses? B.C.'s Year 2000 plan anticipated blending them into "strands" that would reflect the way we actually work. This provoked attacks from the bureaucracy at all levels. When the schools break up knowledge into lots of airtight compartments, more people enjoy power. English Lit becomes one feudal fiefdom; business writing becomes another; word processing becomes a third. The academic petty nobility can then indulge in turf wars and political infighting while avoiding any responsibility for students' development outside the nobility's specific domain.

I'll have something to say later about ways to subvert this system; for now, we could probably get much of this curriculum into the present subject fields if the public demanded it. Anyone with a stake in maintaining the bureaucracy should prod it in this direction; but they will eventually find themselves re-enacting Mikhail Gorbachev's gallant effort to rescue Soviet communism from itself. For much the same reasons they will fail because their system, like Gorbachev's, is based on control of information. Technology is now taking away that control, and the schools will never regain it.

7

Schools and Technology

Meeting Yana and Yevgeni

In the late 1980s I began to get involved with computer-based distance education. It was a slow and clumsy business (at least I was slow and clumsy), but it began to show me what the medium could do.

A professor at Simon Fraser University helped to get me and my article-writing students linked by computer with journalism students at the Bauman Technical Institute in Moscow. We sent our articles (and a lot of my course materials) to the U.S.S.R. by modem. The Novosti press agency translated everything into Russian, and then translated the Russian students' work into English and fired it off to us.

The impact on my students and me was extraordinary. We were suddenly dealing with real people on the other side of the planet. Their articles were vivid glimpses of their own world, like this short piece called "How I Spent Last Tuesday," by a young woman named Yana Tikhonova.

Today is Tuesday. My boyfriend Yevgeni is back from the hospital. He served in Afghanistan and was wounded there. I waited for him for two long years. And finally we are together. I wanted to forget about anything else in the world. No way. On that day I had an exam in computer technology and design.

I thought I knew the subject fairly well. I am a good student but my emotional state ruined all my plans.

Usually I am the first to answer at an exam. This time I was in a hurry because Yevgeni was waiting for me in the street. But the teacher decided to quiz me on the whole course. I answered for forty-five minutes and gave muddled replies because I was so nervous. He gave me an only "satisfactory" mark. It was the first such setback in my five years of studies.

Yevgeni waited for my story but I didn't say a word. I didn't want to disappoint him because he thought so highly of me. We walked along the streets of Moscow, but I couldn't tell him about my bad luck.

In the evening I told my parents all about the exam and they said I should take a second examination.

I couldn't fall asleep for a long time. The day was over. How can a person be so happy and unhappy at the same time?

Now, that article was a gem, but you have to understand that this whole exchange was not private. Everything we put into the sfu computer was accessible to anyone using it, and that computer is open to thousands of educators across the country. Not only were teachers reading these articles, so were their students. So a student at Rosedale Collegiate in Toronto promptly got into the act, offering Yana some heartfelt advice on her relationship with Yevgeni.

In effect a new community, a kind of micro-society, was springing up, composed of Russian and Canadian students and teachers. Its members were just a bunch of teenagers and adults staring into computer monitors; we would never meet most of the people we were communicating with. But we were beginning to share a new sensibility. Before long we learned to call this new medium "cyberspace" and we began to develop that new sensibility into a kind of culture.

Science fiction authors had foreseen something like it, especially in tales of telepathic children who communicate across the world—John Wyndham's *Re-Birth*, a popular novel in Canadian schools for many years, is a good example. But none of us foresaw the impact of such communication technology on education. Let me try to make up for that with a brief science-fiction vignette:

A Virtual Education

The year is 2005—maybe sooner. You're holding a plastic box about the size and thickness of a loose-leaf binder. Half of the face of the box is a screen. Below it is a keyboard, a microphone, and an earphone jack. The whole gadget looks like an outsized Game Boy. You're studying Canadian history, and the binder-sized computer is your teacher/librarian. The screen shows a photograph of Louis Riel. It's a familiar photo, but now it's a colourized, digitized, animated 3-D image. Riel doesn't look "historical" any more; he looks alive.

Now Riel is standing in the dock at his trial, facing a crowded courtroom. In stereo you hear the murmur of the audience, the distant bark of a dog. You hear him speak, see him gesture. Meanwhile the text of his speech appears as subtitles. Along the edge of the screen are small "button" images. You touch one and the speech stops. You press another one, titled "Details," and then touch the images of the other people in the picture. Their names appear beside them. Touching a name fills the screen with a brief biography of the person.

You return to the speech. When it's over you press a button titled "Comment." A bibliography of historical research scrolls up the screen. You can read each article, or skim to another one. You find the name of Gabriel

Dumont in one of the articles. Put your finger on the name and his portrait appears on the screen. The multimedia essay you write about Riel and Dumont will include "buttons" referring your reader to your sources.

Advances in graphics, audio, and computer memory will soon turn this science fiction into everyday reality. Through such computerized teaching students will be able to understand their subjects better than ever before. Going in any direction they like, they'll learn what most concerns them. In a subject like history, they'll see vivid recreations of events.

But such teaching will have its hazards as well. Conditioned by TV, computer learners may expect a certain number of "jolts per minute." Louis Riel's speech, for example, might become a voice-over for an animation of the Battle of Batoche—again with colour, 3-D, and very realistic bloodshed. After that the student might forget all about the issues of the North West Rebellion and go looking for more gory images.

Computer graphics could provide even more jolts. They can already give us "virtual reality." Using goggles with video monitors for lenses, we can step into an electronic hallucination created inside a computer. So you could seem to be standing on the cliffs at Batoche, and by walking around you could watch the battle while listening to Riel's speech.

But what seems most real can be utterly false. Because such computerized "texts" will be so powerful, their accuracy and emphasis will be politically sensitive. (Imagine a "virtual reality" account of the Plains of Abraham or the October Crisis.) So adopting such materials could trigger sharp protests and complaints of brainwashing.

The technology that can present us with such problems is here, or will be within a couple of years. No doubt it will go through a series of buzzwords ("multimedia" is the current favorite, but probably won't last), before settling down as the easiest, most effective way to communicate all kinds of information.

The notebook-sized computer I've described is independent; it contains its own data on a huge scale, but doesn't connect to others. When it does—and it will—it will form a network that will knock down the walls of every classroom in the world. Just as computer networks have made corporate middle management obsolete, they are changing the organization of school as well.

On my home computer one autumn Sunday, I picked up a couple of projects that students had e-mailed to me. I also posted a notice to my Applied Information Technology students at Capilano College about their next assignment. By Monday morning, before coming to school, they'd all read it.

I also spent some time electronically visiting Virtual High, a Vancouver private school whose students work mostly at home. But they can hook up to their school's computer network to exchange information (sometimes at 2:30 in the morning!). These are perfectly typical experiences in education for growing numbers of people. George Gilder, an American writer on technology, has pointed out that computers are linking up into networks at a dramatic rate. The more they do so, the more efficient and valuable they become.

So far, telecomputing faces limits from copper-wire technology and the feeble capacity of most personal computers. But the pace of technological change means we are within sight of something very different.

Gilder notes that since the 1970s, the number of transistors on a silicon chip has doubled about every eighteen months. This means exponential growth in computing power while prices drop. Gordon Moore, the chairman of Intel Corporation, first observed this phenomenon, now known as "Moore's Law." Today's most advanced chips have around 20,000 transistors; by 2003, the doubling rate will mean a billion-transistor chip. In effect, says Gilder, the computing power of sixteen Cray supercomputers (total 1993 cost: $320 million) will be available in 2003 on one chip for under $100. If Moore's Law continues to operate, by 2020 that power will cost about a dime. What's more, millions of personal computers using such chips will be in operation. Each computer will contain both astounding amounts of information and powerful means of shaping that information. And each computer will hook up to millions of others.

TV and even telephones will vanish. Imagine a video link that puts your image on someone else's computer screen for what used to be a phone call. The computer screen could be as small as a compact mirror, or as big as a window.

Your computer will search the network for whatever information it knows you want—old movies, a news summary, a good novel, or statistical data on the number of people who no longer commute to work. Among those ex-commuters will be teachers, students, and school-building construction workers. Face-to-face contacts will still happen, and one of teachers' most important jobs will be to help students avoid the electronic garbage that will clutter the networks. But most education will be independent, self-paced home learning.

After all, why bother going to a school when you have all the resources of the world's great libraries (and some really good teachers) available right at home?

The students at Virtual High come to their school building more often than they need to because, like most teenagers, they enjoy socializing. But they can do just as much at home, learning at their chosen speed and at ungodly hours if they like. Such students are the forerunners of a revolution that will overwhelm ordinary chalk-and-talk schools.

Revolutions, however, don't always turn out the way rev-

olutionaries expect. After all, TV was going to be a great
force for education also. Educational materials certainly
won't improve as fast as the technology will; first a sizable
body of educators has to master the new medium and create appropriate electronic texts. Until then, most school
software will be pretty dreadful. Computerized education
could produce an ironic outcome: cheap, mediocre materials for the poor, while the rich pay heavily for the snob-
appeal luxury of live teachers for their children.

Even with first-rate materials, enormous computer
power won't turn education into a sunny summer weekend
in Utopia. Computers and telecommunications offer some
solutions to present education problems, but they raise new
problems as well. We should be aware of them before we
go much further into high tech.

The potentially worst problem is also the least certain.
If we start children out on computers at an early age, we
may be exposing them to a little-understood danger. Computer monitors give off fairly strong electromagnetic fields,
and they may pose a real health hazard as more children
become computer users. The American author Paul
Brodeur has written several books on the potential threat
of such fields, mostly from power lines, but also from computers. Women in particular may be at risk; Brodeur says
studies show increased rates of miscarriage for women who
work at video display terminals.

Other computer drawbacks, while not life-threatening,
are still serious education problems. Operating from home,
some students go on-line with little desire or incentive to
study systematically. They may use telecommunications
just to gossip or to download software—not to advance
their educations.

Computers will eventually take over much of the repetitive work of teaching. But on-line students will still need
plenty of direct contact with live teachers for guidance,

advice, and encouragement. Those teachers won't be able to handle more than a normal student load, and may need a much lower one.

Diktuphobia: Fear of the Net

Many teachers are coming down with a new kind of fear: *diktuphobia*, or "net fear." They see the Internet, often with reason, as a threat to them, their students, and their whole role in the process of industrial-model education.

Many students start exploring the Internet—a worldwide computer network—only to find much of it is a toxic waste dump. For some users, it's just a convenient source of pornographic pictures and text. People with similar interests form Internet "newsgroups" to discuss them. Not all are healthy. Some push neo-Nazi propaganda. Unsavory cranks and bigots dominate other newsgroups.

Good educational material does exist on the Internet, but it's often hard to find and harder to use. Many Internet-linked computers provide mostly junk—dumb games, useless shareware, and irrelevant databases.

The culture of the Internet isn't always welcoming to young people. Electronic mail and discussions in the newsgroups are sometimes worse than rude. "Flame wars" break out, with combatants using language ranging from the crude to the libellous. An innocent question or comment may trigger an avalanche of abuse. Women using the Internet often find themselves pestered and harassed by electronic lechers. The only way for women to escape unwanted attention is to use initials instead of first names. Even more alarming, some adults go online to seek out children. The purpose is to dump obscene or abusive remarks on the kids' monitors. Schools with their own private bulletin-board systems can keep out such unwelcome intruders, but it's a different story out on the Internet itself.

Yet one of the benefits of the Internet is that it permits

freedom to speak, to read, and to explore. Teachers want to foster those freedoms, but feel caught in a double-bind. A premature encounter with the seamy side of the Net may turn students off for good. Yet closing off some parts of the Net may only make the skinheads and pornographers seem more interesting and attractive. Sooner than try to resolve this paradox, some teachers will prefer to go back to their textbooks.

We have one big encouragement. Used properly, computers in education promote empathy and understanding. If you can't put yourself in your reader's shoes, the computer is a terrible way to communicate. Children already understand that, and the rest of us are learning the lesson too.

For teachers, however, the lesson is not an entirely welcome one. That's because the technology is, in effect, begging the whole question of schools themselves.

When asked why he robbed banks, Willy Sutton replied: "Because that's where the money is." For thousands of years, people have gone to school because that's where the knowledge is. Just preserving it there has usually been a challenge for most societies. Thousands of peasants would have to toil to support a handful of literate clerks and priests whose duties included training their replacements. Control of knowledge meant power, and its flow was vertical.

Our pen-and-paper technology has become "transparent"—something we don't notice because it's so familiar—but it took a long time to get that way. From a skill possessed by a tiny minority, literacy has become the norm. It took half a millenium to achieve our present levels, however, and we educators are still under fire for failing to make literacy universal.

By the same token, those of us who use computers in education are a minority who often find it difficult to bring our colleagues up to even nominal skill levels. Inducing them to use computers in their classrooms is almost impossible, so for most North American educators the computer remains a glorified typewriter—and a very "opaque" technology.

Even the most computer-illiterate educator can see the threat implicit in the technology. For the first time, the flow of knowledge need not be vertical. It is becoming horizontal, and the teacher is far from crucial to its transmission. I saw this, paradoxically, in a failed experiment in computer-mediated instruction. As a mentor in a distance-education writing project, I received students' work from schools all over the British Columbia interior. I would download their work, read it, and upload my detailed comments. It was an exciting and dramatic way to bring students and teachers together, but for some reason we never got to the point of extended dialogue. Nor did I hear from anything like the number of students I had expected, since so many school districts had joined the project.

Not until I met with some of the participants did I learn the real reasons. In one school, uploading messages was the job of a staff person with plenty of other things to do as well. In another, the mentor project was the interest of just one very busy teacher. The students were still at one remove from the process. Moreover, it soon became clear that many teachers felt threatened by students' access to outside information. It implied a freedom from the local curriculum, an ability to define one's own curriculum. The teacher looks increasingly unneeded under those conditions.

The self-defined curriculum is exactly what we now see in bulletin-board systems and Internet newsgroups, where individuals request and send information as they please, and deal with no subject unless they wish to. While organized online courses are growing, the real vigor in the system seems to me to exist in just those anarchic forums, whether dedicated to *Star Trek* or to the latest developments in particle physics.

I feel less confident that teachers will be able to provide appropriate material by incorporating these anarchic online resources into the existing curriculum. Who decides what's appropriate—the teachers or the kids? And for whose agenda—the teachers' or the kids'?

Talking to prisoners at a local penitentiary a couple of years ago, I naïvely expressed the desire that they get online. They laughingly told me the authorities would never grant them access to modems, probably because modems would make the penitentiary walls a "transparent technology" indeed. Someone would surely start robbing banks while still doing time.

Similarly, educators sense that kids with computers are likely to break out into that horizontal knowledge flow, and escape teacher control. Some of us think that breakout is the whole purpose of education, but it still scares most of us to death.

Most proposals for school reform promise all kinds of technology as part of the school furniture, but they don't address a more fundamental issue: the technology is becoming ubiquitous, and the skills are developing among students far faster than they are among teachers. In effect, computers are distributing power among students as well as teachers, and making teachers redundant in the process.

St. Augustine prayed for freedom from lust—"But not yet, O Lord." Teachers similarly pray to make their students independent, lifelong learners who don't need teachers—"But not yet!" For many of us, the power and control we exercise over our students are psychologically rewarding and professionally necessary. If students can define their own curriculum, pursue their own interests, do they really need teachers at all? In Mexico, where literacy is sparse and typewriters are few, public scribes can still earn a living

because people must come to them for everything from
legal documents to love letters. In the U.S. and Canada,
such scribes would starve to death. Today's typical North
American teacher faces a similar fate.

When computers and fiberoptic networks become as
available as a dial tone, students will have little reason to
congregate in one building. When they realize that any
course—any information—is accessible online, the implications will shake the school system to its roots.

In 1990 I taught writing online to students in B.C., Ontario, and Baffin Island in the Canadian Arctic. One Inuk
student in Pond Inlet sent us all a story that has reverber-
ated in cyberspace ever since. "The Struggling Story of
Surusumiitut," by Sue Qitsualik, brought us all "face to
face" with a powerful talent operating in both her own
culture and in ours. At that point she needed access to her
teacher's technology, but by the end of the decade she will
be able to reach literally millions of other individuals without going through an intermediary.

I saw something like that unmediated contact on another occasion when those Russian journalism students,
asking my students about Canadian Indians, got their
answer from some Chilcotin Indian students at Col-
umneetza Senior Secondary in Williams Lake, B.C., who
had been eavesdropping online and decided to join in.
When I saw the Indian students' comments, I felt de-
lightedly superfluous.

Yes, computer technology can and will transform the
schools, but it will be a process that many educators will
resist bitterly because it will also transform their role. As
someone recently observed, the teacher will no longer be
"the mentor at the center or the sage on the stage," but
merely "the guide on the side."

Computers will not automate teachers out of a job in
the classical industrial sense; they will not permit one

teacher to look after five times as many students, and thereby take work away from four other teachers. In my own experience, linking a teacher with a student via computer takes up more time, not less. But the teacher will spend far less time in repetitive tasks like lecturing, and much more in individualized response to individual student needs.

For example, I have explained the functions of the semicolon more times to more people than anyone should have to. Suppose I do it one last time, armed with all the bells and whistles of multimedia, and put my best effort into a digitized computer presentation. Students watch this presentation and do the exercises that go with it, just as they might read a chapter in a textbook and do the exercises at the end. But the multimedia presentation—providing plenty of interactive jolts—is more effective; the students understand semicolons faster.

Of course students have questions. They post these in a discussion group where other students can read them. I respond to the questions as fully as possible. When certain questions become predictable, I build my responses into the original presentation, or into a standard FAQ (Frequently Asked Questions) file that students can consult on their own. Now I'm reserving my real energies for the unpredictable questions and for more interesting issues: once you understand the semicolon's correct use, what influence might it have on style? Are three semicolons in one paragraph too many because they draw attention to themselves, and is such distraction acceptable?

At this point teaching ceases to be vertical; the teacher is not just turning a faucet so that punctuation gushes into the student's head. Instead, two writers are talking shop, and each is likely to benefit from the horizontal exchange of ideas.

Nor is this a vague possibility for a distant future: I

began teaching an online version of a writing course in the fall of 1994, with all the teaching materials available on the computer. Scores of other institutions are already running whole education programs online.

Can you see why many teachers dread such a change in their roles? Historically they have enjoyed a position of superiority over students, purchased at the price of a kind of standardization: Give the students a chalk-and-talk lecture, often with the same examples and jokes year after year, and you exert power over them.

Oh, you may update the examples and jokes, like a standup comic polishing material. But it's really just the same stuff the kids could get out of the book if the book weren't so boring. You've endured the boredom of mastering the material, and now you're jazzing it up to make it more palatable—but you're still really just repeating it. Put the entertainment straight into the information, and what's left for the teacher? You're not just *teaching* math or geography or history; now, when you deal with your students, you *are* a mathematician, a geographer, a historian. And so are they, even if on a less sophisticated level. They're not subordinates any more; they're *colleagues*. The computer has distributed some of your power to them.

I suspect that many teachers find that a deeply unsettling thought. And if computers are going to take over the routine aspects of their job, and leave them with nothing but the requirement to improvise intelligently and sensitively, many teachers are going to fight computers to the last ditch.

Teachers' psychological need for control is largely a function of the industrial-model school, which has always fostered a hierarchy of such controllers. The model set out to train order-taking employees for an industrial economy, and like factories and armies, the model fostered a culture of control. Naturally the system recruits and rewards teachers who accept the model and its culture.

Unsurprisingly, the hierarchy always finds reasons to prolong education—first to high school graduation, then to college, now to post-graduate degrees. As we'll see in the next chapter, when you prolong education you prolong control.

The Internet-based school, however, will develop a different culture and recruit a very different kind of teacher. The function of the online educator will be to save students from wasting time, to set some intriguing challenges, and to get students out of the academic nest as quickly as possible. To foster freedom, responsibility, and initiative will demand that teachers themselves display those three traits.

Frightening though it may seem to contemplate the end of the old chalk-and-talk school system, we at least have timing on our side. A whole generation of teachers is about to retire; the schools built for the baby boomers are in need of replacement. But we don't have to reconstruct the whole system, least of all if it's obsolete.

The Internet is a kind of planetary schoolhouse staffed by millions of teachers. We can enroll our children (and ourselves) in it with a few keystrokes or mouse clicks. If we look at the Internet as an enormous resource, not as a threat, diktuphobia will soon join smallpox as a disease without victims.

8

The Role of Post-Secondary Education

A couple of years ago I became a western Canada recruiter for my alma mater, Columbia University. This did not greatly add to my workload, but it advanced my own education considerably.

For half my life I've been teaching English courses in a suburban Vancouver community college. We serve a varied population, from affluent West Van white kids to Native Indians to Iranians to working-class East Vancouverites. Many are fresh from high school while many others have been out of school for decades. Some are smart, some are dull, but they're all pretty engaging. I like them a lot and I'm proud that some have become my colleagues, teaching at Capilano and other community colleges.

Very few of them, however, are like the students I interview for Columbia. While a handful are applying only because their fathers are rich and ambitious, in general they are far beyond even the best of our teenage students. They have learned more in high school (whether public or private), enjoyed richer family lives, and appear astonishingly poised for such young people. They clearly expect a great deal from life, and from themselves; had people like these been competing with me for places in Columbia's class of 1962, I wouldn't have had a chance.

I confess I felt a little envious of their future teachers: keeping ahead of such kids would be an intellectual challenge in itself. But while I was sorry not to be teaching them, I felt even sorrier for the students. Wherever they ended up—Columbia, Harvard, Stanford, McGill—their education was going to cost them and their families (and the taxpayers) a fortune. They would get a shot at a superb education only because their parents or grandparents could afford to pay as much as $25,000 a year to put them through.

And yet, paradoxically, even their educations would suffer because of the enormous size of North America's post-secondary system. Size means an ever-growing administrative structure, ever-changing demands from new groups entering post-secondary, and the dilution of genuine scholarship by the sheer scale of academic activities.

The college where I teach is itself a result of post-secondary hypertrophy. Vancouver in the mid-1960s was just an overgrown sawmill town, but popular demand for more access to education was growing yearly. In response, the provincial government built Simon Fraser University and founded the first handful of community colleges.

Intellectual development of students was not a strong motive among educators then. I well recall an administrator in my first job pointing out that we were training young people for essentially boring jobs, so our teaching methods better get them accustomed to it. Whether he knew it or not, that administrator understood something: the education we were offering (and still offer) is not Oxford 1925 on a larger scale. It is an elaborate, time-consuming rite of passage for people lacking scholarly backgrounds, values, and interests. It may sometimes test knowledge, skill, and intellectual talent, but it mostly tests patience, stamina, affluence, and the ability to defer gratification. Those who pass those tests go into a relatively small pool of candidates for professional and semiprofessional jobs; those who fail must seek less prestigious occupations.

"Relatively small" is still pretty big. According to Statistics Canada, the number of post-secondary full-time students has increased ninefold in forty years—from 91,000 in 1951 to 857,000 in 1990. Another half a million were studying part-time, and international students added another 35,000.

All these students are distributed among over 270 post-secondary institutions, most of them in Ontario and Quebec. In 1991 those schools employed 63,520 full-time faculty—25,000 in the colleges and the rest in the universities—plus unknown thousands of part-timers and support staff. The median salary for full-time faculty ranged in 1989 from $66,650 for a full professor to $41,400 for assistant professors. Community college instructors' median salary was $44,877.

To support this gigantic enterprise, Canada spent $13.5 billion in 1990—in constant 1986 dollars, eighteen times the $80 million it spent in 1951. As a result we have a higher rate of enrollment than any other developed nation except the U.S.: sixty-two percent of all persons aged twenty to twenty-four, compared to the Americans' sixty-seven percent. The average of fourteen other developed countries in the 1980s was only thirty-one percent.

The post-secondary system drives the whole public-school curriculum, but we don't always think about what exactly drives post-secondary itself. In this chapter I want to deal not with specifics (the best electrical-engineering program, the worst grade inflation) but with the "anthropology" of post-secondary education. The culture of colleges and universities, both here and in the United States, staggers under the same heavy burdens that afflict the public schools; the same mistaken premises about equality and disparity have led to an entrenched bureaucracy, enormous wastes of time and energy, and a system that serves neither scholarship nor the workplace except by accident. Post-secondary education has become just another racket.

The Twilight Of Credentialism

Sometimes a new idea, especially one with a moral overtone, strikes people as manifestly absurd and contrary to common sense. Tell your two-year-old she should share her toys, and she looks at you as if you'd gone mad. Tell your fifteen-year-old he should respect women, and he snorts sarcastically while dismissing you as a hopeless fool.

The child's agenda is to gain all possible power; ideas like sharing toys or respecting women imply losing power to someone else. That's a threatening and subversive implication, and it usually succeeds only when put in terms of gaining still more power: share your toys and you can use your playmates' toys. Show respect to women and you'll succeed with more of them.

As adults, our agenda usually includes a continued search for power, and sharing it—with the poor, with women, with ethnic minorities, with animals—is as unpopular with us as it is with two-year-olds. So I do not expect my fellow educators to welcome the ideas that follow. They derive, after all, from the cautious premise that we enjoy entirely too much power over students and society, and we should relinquish a great deal of it. We wield our power because we set the terms for everyone's entry into the working world: we can give or withhold a piece of paper called a diploma or degree—a credential.

Lewis Perelman raises the issue of credentialism in a recent book called *School's Out: Hyperlearning, the New Technology and the End of Education*. Perelman argues that as long as you must have an academic degree or diploma to get a decent job, the education system has you over a barrel.

To the extent that we educators think about it at all, it's only to rejoice that God has so wisely provided us with the barrel. The rest of the population is less delighted with this divine ordinance, but they accept it without question. Indeed, belief in the value of a piece of paper is so ingrained that most people consider credentialism a solution instead of a problem.

The problem with dropouts, after all, is not that they're incompetent; the problem is that *they don't have their Grade 12 diploma*. The problem with post-secondary education is that *too many people can't get in to obtain a degree*. Too many others fail to complete their BA, MA, or PHD. So despite their expensive schooling they don't qualify for demanding jobs.

However, their incomplete education may overqualify them for joe jobs. And even if they do stay the course, employment is scarce. Statistics Canada found that in 1987 almost a third of the BA graduates of 1982 were underemployed, and over half of the 1982 MA's were also underemployed.

With stoic passivity, generations of Canadians and Americans have accepted this state of affairs. I doubt that a single family in North America has escaped its influence. Certainly mine did not. My father, the only son of rather bohemian parents, entered school at age ten and left at fifteen. A year later he was the youngest licenced radio operator in the United States, working as such on a freighter to Scandinavia. He later became an actor, an inventor, an air traffic controller, a TV engineer (he trained the entire staff of a large Mexican TV station), a TV scriptwriter, and the sound man for a TV news crew. He was an exceedingly well-read man, with informed interests in science, history, politics, and social issues. Yet his lack of even a high-school diploma deterred him from seeking many jobs, and he saw himself as a failure because of his lack of formal education.

In that he was typical of his generation, and typical also

in making sure that his children pursued their educations as far as possible. The enormous expansion of post-secondary education in the 1950s and 1960s was a direct result of the parental dreams of the generation that grew up in the Depression and fought in the Second World War.

I suppose I should be grateful for that parental encouragement; it pushed me beyond my own ambitions into Columbia. I was not a very good student, but I emerged with a BA. This piece of paper was to change my life.

First it got me a clerk-typist's job in the U.S. Army. That is, it qualified me to take a typing test in an administration unit at Fort Ord. My speed as a self-taught typist, not my BA in English, got me a job cutting the orders that sent other poor bastards to Vietnam. On my release I found another clerical job, for which I appeared to be overqualified, so my superiors kindly found me work as an apprentice technical writer-editor. Close critical study of John Donne and Thomas DeQuincey had not prepared me for this kind of work, and while I could do it I did not enjoy it. So when the idea of emigrating to Canada occurred to my wife and me, we decided to try new careers in a new country.

Incredible as it now seems, MA's in English were rare in B.C. when I applied for my first teaching job at Vancouver Community College in 1967. VCC would have much preferred someone with a master's, but at least I had that BA from Columbia; the person who hired me had taken courses there too, and the fall semester was only two weeks away.

The work was a great deal of fun, although again it had nothing to do with what I had studied in New York. Instead I was drawing on my experience in organizing technical reports—for which I had no formal training and certainly no certificate.

When I moved to Capilano College the next year, my new employers made it clear I would need more of a credential if I wanted a long-term job. Accordingly, I entered an MA program at Simon Fraser. My thesis, in Canadian literature, provoked a nasty squabble among my committee because they couldn't agree on the proper format for my footnotes, but I did collect the master's. While I have very rarely taught Canlit since then (the last time was in China in 1983), the degree has qualified me to teach punctuation and business writing for over twenty glorious years.

My wife, meanwhile, had to enter the Vancouver teaching force on a "letter of permission" because the local teacher factory at UBC didn't recognize her lifetime teaching credential from California. I have often reflected on the odd fact that she was barred from a permanent teaching job although formally trained for it, while I gained such a job through graduate work that had nothing to do with teaching methods or with the kind of courses I teach.

I cite my own family's experience not because it is unusual but because it is all too typical. If anyone enters postsecondary with the hope of receiving an education, that hope soon flies; what is important is the piece of paper, and it justifies almost any personal degradation—lays for A's, drug-enhanced cramming for pointless exams, plagiarism, and following proper footnote format.

During the days when the U.S. drafted its young men into the "peacetime" army, apologists for the draft argued that the presence of so many non-professionals tended to "civilianize" the army. The real effect, as I learned to my sorrow, was to militarize the civilian population, which soon took for granted that the armed forces should have anything (and anyone) they wanted. Similarly, the presence on campus of so many involuntary scholars has not made academic life more humane or practical; it has only taught growing numbers of young people to accept arbitrary demands from a privileged class—the professors—whose status and income are clearly unrelated to their work. The explicit reason for obeying these demands is to become similarly privileged. This attitude, carried back into the non-academic world, has strengthened North America's anti-cultural fondness for hierarchy and contempt for productivity—to say nothing of its even greater contempt for intellectual pursuits.

Nevertheless, millions of North Americans scramble for some kind of certification. Ironically, the increase in numbers of high school and college graduates has devalued their achievement. High school graduation once qualified young people for all kinds of work; by 1965 or so, it was just a ticket for further training.

A bachelor's degree, in the last decade or so, has suffered similar devaluation. Many new BA's go right back to school to acquire either an advanced degree or certifiable job training. StatsCan found in 1988 that half of all college and BA graduates re-enrolled in another education program within two years of graduation; so did thirty-five percent of MA graduates and fifteen percent of PHDS.

As each piece of paper becomes less helpful, another piece of paper becomes essential. Like small nations caught up in an arms race they can't afford, young people must now compete furiously with one another to qualify for the next stage of their education.

They are competing on an epic and growing scale. According to Statistics Canada, our 856,500 students in 1990-91 were a three percent increase over the previous year, and 213,000 more than in 1980. In 1989 we granted 82,500 college diplomas, about 105,000 bachelor's degrees, over 16,000 master's degrees and 2,600 PHDS. StatsCan finds that while we endure a fairly high dropout rate from high school, a third of all adult Canadians have some kind of post-secondary credential.

Post-secondary institutions respond to this hysterical market by puffing themselves up and engaging in their own arms race with one another. Community colleges are no longer content to offer just one- or two-year programs;

now they must offer degree programs, preferably as "university colleges." Their principals have become presidents, their deans have become vice-presidents, and all are trying to make their own institutions competitive in their powers of credentialing.

As a result of this arms race, growing numbers of students must commit the entire first third of their lives to the schooling they supposedly need for rewarding employment, which they need so they can pay back their enormous debts and accumulate enough money to live on in retirement. They and their families must sacrifice to afford the cost of study, and the whole society must tax itself heavily to subsidize the hundreds of thousands who—without a credential—would be unemployable.

They are often unemployable in any case. I recently saw the resumé of a young man with a BA in history from a reputable Canadian university; his job history was a string of menial posts, culminating in "server's helper" in a Vancouver restaurant. A young woman with a new master's in journalism applied to me for a teaching job; no newspapers would hire her, and she had not, apparently, reflected on the wisdom of teaching others to follow her career path. In any case I had no job for her, and at last report she was off to teach English in Japan. Other applications come to me from people in their thirties or forties, with advanced degrees and no related work experience apart from a little sessional teaching.

Despite the growing numbers of such unemployable graduates, governments foster ever more belief in credentialism. Official reports predict that for the foreseeable future, new jobs will require seventeen years' formal schooling—the equivalent of a master's degree. Politicians warn of the dire consequences of high-school dropouts, of uncompleted college educations: the better-credentialed Japanese and Germans will outdo us economically. And both Canadian and American census figures indicate that a degree can indeed mean a difference of hundreds of thousands of dollars—sometimes millions—in lifetime earnings.

Yet for all that we seemingly need advanced education to stay competitive, our credentialed workers are manifestly incapable of sustaining prosperity. In 1988 alone, Canadian universities awarded almost 3,000 master's and doctor's degrees in commerce; those graduates have spent most of their careers under recession conditions. Another 3,000 received advanced degrees in education that year, and never has the public been less happy with the schools than in the last five years.

As most educated people will recognize, this is the *argumentum ad bolsum*—the argument to the purse, a crass equation of learning and money. Surely we send our children off to school to become not just better paid, but better people.

Does the experience of advanced education really enlighten and ennoble anyone? Not to judge from the behaviour and rhetoric now common on North American campuses. Consider the number of sexual-harassment charges made against professors, or the number of racist, sexist, violent, unethical or illegal incidents that occur routinely. (Columbia University now presents a daily list of campus security incidents on its computer system.) Gossip in any faculty lounge portrays a wretched population of philandering spouses, incompetent teachers, careerist bureaucrats, mediocre researchers, and the kinds of students such role models would attract. Intellectual discussion in such a venue, while not impossible, is unlikely; debate usually focuses on more urgent issues like parking and office space. Of course most faculty members are smart, humane, admirable people; but their formal education did not make them that way.

So academic credentials do not guarantee usable job skills, or even basic decency. The schools that produce credentialed graduates have become a kind of sunset industry;

they are obsolete, expensive, and inefficient, yet their managers and workers would only be a worse nuisance if they were cast loose to seek an honest living.

Credentialism is not an innate flaw in education, but a result of the misuse we have made of it. Post-secondary education in particular should be dedicated to the pursuit of scholarship for its own sake—whether in high-energy physics, biology or Chaucer. But we have made scholarship (better said, the certified pretence of it) into a prerequisite for utterly unrelated kinds of work outside the academy, and credentialism is the result. The scholars themselves have co-operated in this abuse of scholarship. Floods of state-subsidized students bring in money for research, for teaching assistants, for secretaries, for offices and labs and travel. The price scholars pay is to teach (as little as possible) large numbers of young people who could not care less about their subjects. A few students may be potentially good apprentices, but finding them is a tedious business.

To ease the apprentice-spotting process, the scholars pressure the public schools to "improve academic standards"—regardless of the impact of ordinary, non-scholarly young people who just want to make a living, and a life, free of footnotes. Perelman observes that today's education is really just vocational training for the job of college professor; yet we make everyone train for it.

Consider an analogy. Suppose we collectively decided that we would give the best jobs and highest prestige to sprinters. Track coaches would find themselves awash in money, but only if they accepted countless students who could barely stagger. The coaches would have to work with swarms of young stumblers in Remedial Walking courses, all the while proclaiming "Excellence in Sprinting." (The junior coaches, that is; the senior coaches would be away at conferences on track surfacing, locker-room design, and building sprinter self-esteem.)

With their enhanced incomes at stake, coaches would soon find ways to pass even their hopeless students. Special educational stopwatches would run slow, granting plodders a chance to run to glory. Educators would debate the exact definition of "100 meters": before long, ninety meters would be close enough. Maybe eighty-five. Steroids would become mandatory. After all, if they flunked too many student sprinters, it would look bad and the kids wouldn't get jobs.

The only threat to this pleasant existence for coaches would be for employers to hire non-sprinters anyway. That wouldn't happen, thank heaven, because employers would have to stay "competitive" with firms that hired only sprinters.

Absurd, of course—but no more absurd than to suppose an apprentice literary critic or sociologist is more employable than someone who never heard of Walter Pater or C. Wright Mills. Yet employers still prefer applicants who have undergone such an apprenticeship.

This reflects badly on employers' trust in their own judgment. A degree, as they loudly and rightly complain, is no proof of competency—least of all when they themselves hold one, or the economy might be stronger. But demanding a degree cuts down on the number of applicants. In the old days, hiring on the basis of race, sex or nationality served the same purpose. Lewis Perelman rightly calls credentialism a civil-rights issue. The law, he says, shouldn't allow employers to discriminate in favor of people with degrees.

Suppose we grant Perelman's point, that employers should hire strictly on the basis of demonstrated ability to do the job. A credential, by definition, gives the employer grounds to *believe* the applicant is capable. Reject credentials, and what can you believe in apart from the applicant's self-serving claims?

Perelman would replace the Grade 12 diploma with a

"Certificate of Basic Competency" (CBC)—a guarantee that graduates have at least entry-level work skills. Of course, you wouldn't need to wait until Grade 12 to acquire your CBC if you could pass the test sooner. And you'd be crazy to leave school without it.

But who would design the CBC test? As long as the testing authority was independent of educators, it could be an employers' group or a government agency. The Motor Vehicle Branch, after all, doesn't care if you learned to drive from your mother or from a driving school. You earn your licence when you prove you can drive, not because your mother is rich or the driving school has ivy-covered walls.

The CBC, like your driver's licence, would say nothing about your understanding of Shakespeare's sonnets, your fluency in Spanish or your knowledge of plant biology. It would measure only the basic abilities that employers would like to see in young workers. These would presumably include rapid reading, clear and correct writing, listening, speaking, and numeracy.

That is actually a fairly modest level of skill, and many could attain it by Grade 8. It doesn't mean, however, that fourteen-year-olds are going to flood onto the job market. They would recognize that "basic" means just that— enough to qualify for pushing a broom. Besides, they would still have to master the knowledge, skills, and attitudes required of fully competent citizens.

Beyond the basics, then, job seekers could obtain specialized skills from public or private schools, or as apprentices. They might obtain certificates of completion, but the real ticket would again come from an independent judging body.

Employers could of course run their own tests, perhaps after in-house training. They would have an obvious interest in first-rate training and accurate assessment. And in many cases they might well decide that a background in the liberal arts would indeed be a basic competency. If so, students would have to turn back to Shakespeare and the Brontës, and to prepare for testing on the pre-Raphaelites or Mozart.

This may sound like a contradiction of my earlier suggestions about a core curriculum emphasizing the arts, history, religion, and other non-economic subjects. The public schools should demand more than "basic competency" because they are also educating young people for a civic role. But we are dealing, in post-secondary, with very little more than job training and personal interest. To the extent that the public must subsidize post-secondary education, it should have a say in what it subsidizes—and leave study for personal interest to individuals who can pay for it.

Could we break the grip of credentialism? The idea seems daunting. Yet one recent case suggests it can be done. China for centuries ran its affairs with the help of a credentialed class of mandarins. An elaborate system of schools and examinations worked to staff the empire's bureaucracy. The system survived warlords, invasions, communist takeover, and even the Cultural Revolution.

The Chinese economic boom, however, has done what Mao's Red Guards could not: made credentialed education almost worthless. Canadian educator Robert Cosbey, who has taught all over China since the 1970s, reports that the country's graduate programs are frantically lowering standards in an effort to attract students. Even women are now allowed into hitherto male-only disciplines. The reason? A bachelor's or advanced degree leads only to a monthly salary of perhaps $30 Canadian; a job in the booming private sector can pay ten times as much regardless of certification. China's best and brightest are therefore deserting the schools that were once their only hope of security and prestige.

Similarly, but more consciously, Perelman's civil-rights approach would reduce the economic advantage of a credential, and deprive education of its present captive market.

Far from destroying the schools, the end of credentialism would rescue them from their present bureaucratic stagnation. The system would become smaller, simpler, and more productive. Many who now drop out would rip through school in record time, grab their certificates, and take off for work or further training.

Post-secondary education costs would fall sharply for a good reason: the state would subsidize only the training demanded by the workplace. If students wanted to take other courses out of personal interest or for the good of their souls, they could do so at their own expense.

Universities would therefore shrink into small groups of scholars; they would teach only students who wanted to become scholars also. They might enjoy fewer secretaries, labs, and foreign conferences, but they would also be truly free to study whatever they damn well pleased. Of course their research budgets would be smaller, but consider the progress made in science, technology, and the humanities during the first half of this century, when academics had very little money indeed—and much smaller empires to oversee.

Recalling the years before the Second World War brings another insight. The present education system seems so huge, complex, and entrenched that we forget it is largely a creation of the last forty years—particularly a creation of the Cold War. The economic, political, and technological conditions that gave it life are changing before our eyes. From a kind of "monoculture" of education, we are moving rapidly into a rainforest model of diverse but equally valid approaches to teaching and learning. Their common purpose would not be the production of employees, but of free men and women who choose their own lives, on their own terms.

We can look forward to a system in which education happens everywhere, all the time, to everyone. In that happy time, those who take a historian's interest in late 20th-century educators will say that we were, in more senses than one, certifiable.

The Big Rock Candy Campus

Academic giantism brings other problems as well. The billions of dollars we spend on post-secondary have made it an attractive career not only for academics but also for various kinds of support staff. As I noted earlier, educational institutions are often the biggest employers in their communities and therefore vital to economic stability. They also absorb thousands of young people who would otherwise be looking for some kind of work.

Post-secondary educators have generally been serious in trying to make their schools more accessible to the whole population. This is because we are good, decent people inspired by the confident vision, but it also conveniently enables us to ask for more money to meet unmet student demand. So we go out actively recruiting new customers, bolstering our demands for bigger budgets and more encompassing programs. (The government doesn't always buy it; in 1993, B.C. advanced-education bureaucrats were actually doing headcounts in college classrooms to verify the numbers supposedly in attendance.)

Women, minorities, gays, and the disabled all have enormous potential contributions to make to scholarship. Unfortunately, post-secondary is now far more concerned about processing students than with scholarship; as I just observed, the students bring in money and money brings in privilege and status.

You can see the results in any issue of *The Chronicle of Higher Education*, a weekly American newspaper about events in academe. Half the paper is job listings. Many of them are for bureaucratic posts within the administration, particularly jobs overseeing affirmative-action programs or the specific needs of women and minorities. The rest are teaching jobs, all labelled as going preferentially to women, minorities, gays, and the disabled.

Canadian periodicals like *CAUT Bulletin* display similar ads for similar posts. In the October 1994 issue of *University Affairs*, Dalhousie University advertised for a professor of Black Canadian Studies—and specified that the position was open to blacks only. On the facing page was the magazine's ad policy, reminding readers of human-rights laws that forbid racial discrimination in hiring.

This is the employment-equity issue. I touched on it earlier as the "representative fallacy," but it deserves fuller attention because equity threatens to deprive post-secondary institutions of any real scholarly credibility. When the issue arose on my own campus in 1992, I responded with the argument that follows. The key points of the proposal I was rebutting should be clear from the context.

On an Equity Policy for Capilano College

We in the College face some critical decisions about proposed new policies for hiring and promoting faculty, staff, and administration, and for teaching our students. The recent report of the Equity Committee throws a useful light on the nature of those decisions, and it is now up to the College community to explore the implications of equity.

It is probably a sad reflection on the current political climate that I feel obliged to set out something of my background before discussing the report. As a college student in the U.S., I began my involvement in the civil rights movement with the march on Washington in 1959. After graduation I became an active member of the Congress of Racial Equality. In addition to having taught at Capilano College since its inception in 1968, I am also the author of three books about minorities, women, and education in British Columbia: *Go Do Some Great Thing: The Black Pioneers of British Columbia* (1978); *Exploring British Columbia's Past* (1983), a textbook which emphasizes the roles of

Native Indians and women in the growth of the province; and *School Wars: The Assault on B.C. Education* (1985).

Since 1982 I have written a weekly column (usually on education issues) for the Vancouver *Province*. In it I have repeatedly called for improved access to education for women and minorities. I have urged young women to consider careers in science, and pointed out the financial consequences they face if they drop out of school. So I do not believe I have any apologies to make about my attitude towards racism and sexism. It is precisely because I oppose racist and sexist behaviour that I find fault with the Equity Committee's report.

I first take issue with the report's assumption that some kind of gender bias exists at all in the College. The report cites employment data about the sex, age, employment status, and degree attainments of faculty. Insofar as this data applies to me and my Communications department, it is surprisingly inaccurate; I, for example, appear as a landed immigrant nineteen years after having become a Canadian citizen, and the MA degree of another faculty member is unacknowledged.

Even if these data were accurate in all details, the details are oversimplified. The backgrounds of faculty, like those of everyone else, reflect decisions taken and lived with over many years, for which the College has little or no responsibility. Let me offer an analogy:

When the College opened in 1968, qualified instructors were relatively scarce. Like most other Canadian post-secondary schools in that expansionary time, Capilano College was obliged to hire numerous American, British, and other non-Canadian faculty. Some Canadian-born academics at the time were strenuous critics of such hirings, claiming that Canadians were suffering discrimination. In today's terms, the argument would have been a demand for "citizenship equity."

The fact was, however, that our post-secondary system

had simply not yet produced enough people both qualified and interested in college teaching; indeed, that lack was itself a good reason for expanding the system. As time passed, however, I had the pleasure of seeing some of my former students become colleagues, both here and at other colleges.

These students, like other instructors, had to make a series of decisions and to follow through on them: to go on for a BA, and then for a graduate degree; to choose a teaching career; to apply for positions; to perform well in those positions. Had they chosen to forego graduate school, or to open a business instead of applying for a teaching job, they could hardly expect to make a career in the colleges.

Similarly, many women face decisions that may preclude certain kinds of careers: to have children and stay home with them, for example, or to avoid studying math and science, or to work in a dead-end job so that a partner can gain an education and enter a profession. No doubt many women justifiably resent the pressures that push them to such decisions, but ultimately they make those choices. To argue otherwise is to deprive them of adult responsibility.

To step out of a career path for any reason, and then to complain that one cannot continue with the career at one's convenience, seems to me simply unrealistic. Yet it appears likely that most of the disproportion in male-female appointments stems from conscious decisions taken by women to interrupt their careers—not from some "systemic" bias of the "dominant male culture" against women.

When we consider systemic bias, in the College or any other organization, we are dealing with explicit policies, not implicit ones or unwritten laws. The College has an explicit systemic bias in favor of hiring teachers with post-graduate degrees or extensive specialized work experience. It has an explicit bias against rewarding plagiarism. It explicitly values some kinds of work, like administration and teaching, over other kinds of work like clerical tasks. This is not because the College doesn't like women or minorities, but because it must pay more to attract those with relatively rare skills.

Equity's defenders might define "systemic" as a set of unwritten, implicit assumptions that middle-aged credentialed white males make about academic qualifications: that only Credentialed White Males can really do the job. If that stereotype were true, we CWM's would spend less time gossiping about one another's wretched incompetence. In my experience, we don't have the luxury of choosing only males from the available qualified applicants; we choose the best we can get, and our criteria have nothing to do with anatomical details.

It follows that a dubious premise about the College's gender bias leads to unacceptable conclusions. The draft policy of the Equity Report presents serious difficulties. To comment briefly on the major problems:

- Establishing practices that "do not limit an individual's *or group's* right to employment opportunities for reasons unrelated to ability." (My emphasis.) This is a meaningless concept. All members of a group could not qualify for employment unless all, *as individuals,* hold proper qualifications for a particular job. No group or individual can enjoy a right to employment that by definition must depend on training and experience.
- Correcting "the conditions of disadvantage in employment experienced by designated groups: women, aboriginal peoples, persons with disabilities, persons . . . in a visible minority. . . ." The report does not make clear who is to "designate" those groups, or how. Nor do we see a reasonable definition of those groups. Is a Bosnian "visible" to a Serb? Are severely myopic persons disabled? Is a person who is three-quarters English and one-quarter Haida an "aboriginal" person?

- Correcting the same conditions for "persons who, because of their sexual orientation or beliefs, suffer prejudice or disadvantage in employment." If we take this at face value, men who *believe* in exploiting teenage prostitutes should suffer no discrimination; neither should those who *believe* in fondling five-year-olds, or those who *believe* women really want to be raped. And persons who *believe* homosexuality is a moral failing should find that no bar to employment even though they may have to deal with homosexual colleagues and students.

- College procedures should "eliminate, redress and prevent disadvantage" for designated groups. "Redress" ought to apply only to specific individuals who suffer unfair treatment as College employees or students, and for them we have detailed grievance procedures in our collective agreements and policies. I do not see how the College can "redress" injustices suffered elsewhere, for which it is not responsible. Still less can it redress injustices suffered by some people by hiring or promoting other people who happen to be of the same sex or race or sexual orientation.

The report's proposals for student equity would be more persuasive if they were more precise. "Equal opportunity to achieve maximum potential" is meaningless unless we know what constitutes an equal opportunity and what each student's "potential" may be. If "equal opportunity" means giving all students the same amount of time and attention regardless of their learning abilities or personal circumstances, then some will get more than they need and others will get much less.

Moreover, "potential" in some fields may remain only that, as students dedicate their efforts to achieving their potential in others. One may have potential as a musician, yet choose instead to dedicate oneself to physics or poetry. When the report asks us "to establish, realize and monitor equal opportunity for all applicants to the college so that student enrollment in all programs is diversified to the greatest possible extent," I want to know what "diversified" means. If it means admitting less able students at the expense of the more able, then it is self-contradictory; the "opportunity" is less equal for students who unfortunately resemble the majority attracted to a given program.

For example, a Native Indian male with a poor grade point average might gain admission to Early Childhood Education while a non-visible Polish-born female, with better grades, is denied a seat in the program. That might "diversify" ECE enrollments, but not to anyone's real benefit. Similarly, should a program admit only the first three of eight Sikhs who apply, even if all are qualified, for the sake of ensuring greater ethnic diversity in the total enrollment?

For the same reason, the College cannot create "an environment that asserts the personal worth and dignity of each individual" if equity discriminates in favor of "designated groups." By definition, persons in designated groups are worth more.

If the Equity Committee wishes to free "all programs and curricula" of discriminatory biases, then most courses in literature, history, and philosophy face radical changes. Any writer who appears discriminatory would have to go; we might also find ourselves teaching a "balanced" curriculum of sexually and ethnically "representative" authorities, regardless of their significance within a given discipline. We might think it absurd to teach Maya mathematics as a counterbalance to the Eurocentric mathematics that now dominates the curriculum. But the curriculum in the social sciences and humanities is under attack as a "canon" of Dead White European Males whose thought and art only oppress today's women and minorities.

I will leave it to members of the Office and Technical Employees Union to comment on the section dealing with their concerns, but I do have some observations on the faculty concerns. I share its worries about "redressing systematic discrimination from the past," and about defining equity itself. I do not accept the implicit assumption in the faculty section that the College ought to provide some kind of workplace Utopia for the "total person."

We are in the business of teaching students and doing so with a limited budget in a competitive market. If we offer good working conditions, we attract and hold good employees; if we try to create a workers' paradise, we do so at our students' expense. Nor do I accept that the College is "penalizing" employees regarding pensions or seniority, when the employees' decisions are the actual influence on those issues.

I have often criticized the policies of the community colleges towards part-time temporary faculty. Temps have suffered a quarter-century of poor pay, uncertain employment, and reduced opportunities for professional development—and all this even though they provide most of the elasticity in the system. Without them we would go into administrative paralysis.

But by the same token, eliminating the temporary category would paralyze us also. If we had to offer all temps "ongoing contracts or some kind of 'tenure-track' position," we would find it impossible to hire new people as our programs' faculty requirements changed. Certainly we should pay our temps according to their qualifications, and we should regularize them more quickly than we now do. (We should realize, however, that improving pay and security may also make their jobs more attractive to qualified males, increasing competition for temporary positions.) But if we cannot hire and release at least a few instructors on short notice, the whole system will lock up.

One of the last faculty concerns threatens the credibility of the whole report: The argument that the College is discriminating against women by "hiring 'over-qualified' faculty or advertising 'PHD Preferred' during faculty recruitment. This tendency," the report goes on, "inherently limits women's access to teaching positions at the College, since discriminatory practices result in the production of fewer female PHD's; but more to the point, excellence in teaching is irrelevant to the criterion of the qualification."

Better said, the PHD requirement inherently limits everyone's access to some kinds of teaching positions requiring proof of advanced scholarship. If the PHD is a requirement for university-transfer courses, then our UT program will suffer a severe loss of credibility when we reject male PHD's in favor of females with MA's or even bachelors' degrees. I cannot imagine that the Equity Committee would wish to see universities regard the College as an academically weak institution, but to discriminate against scholars—in a place dedicated to scholarship—would scarcely be in the interests of the women and minorities the Committee is trying to help.

Having said all this, it will come as no surprise that I do not accept the Committee's proposal that we hire an Equity Officer. Educators have an unfortunate habit of identifying a problem and then hiring a non-teacher (who usually doesn't have the problem) to deal with it. This generates a constantly growing bureaucracy, takes a slice of the budget, and increases the numbers of meetings and reports, but rarely solves the problem. Of course, if the problem remains unsolved, then we will have to hire more bureaucrats, hold more meetings, and write more reports. That means less time for teaching, for preparation, for meeting with students, for professional development—never mind the existing level of administrivia imposed upon us by our current problem-solvers.

I hope I am not being cynical in observing that any intelligent Equity Officer would always find something to do. Having identified bias in this or that department or policy, the EO would then presumably oversee its correction and make sure it stayed corrected. The EO would thus become a campus commissar, constantly ensuring that the right percentages of "targeted groups" were on the payroll and class lists, that memos used no sexist language, that the curriculum was free of references to Nigger Jim in *Huckleberry Finn* or the sexual harassment of Nurse Duckett in *Catch-22*.

In all these respects, the EO would be very much like the campus political officers I saw in China. These persons (rarely educators themselves) made sure that students expressed only acceptable views, monitored faculty behavior, and saw to it that students from "good class backgrounds" didn't suffer, because of their peasant upbringing, in comparison with academically stronger students from educated urban families. A bad report from one's political officer would lead first to public criticism (a serious matter indeed) and perhaps to work assignments in Tibet or the western deserts.

"Noncompliance with equity must have consequences," the Equity Report concludes; they might not include a teaching post in Lhasa, but they would certainly be unpleasant consequences for anyone concerned about academic freedom.

Responsible people in the College have told me that if we do not adopt an equity policy, the government will force one upon us. That may well be true, though it sounds like the old advice (no longer acceptable) to relax and enjoy it. And if the Committee's proposal is unacceptable to me, I'd better be able to offer an acceptable alternative. Perhaps the following will help:

- Recognize that we help groups only by helping individuals.
- Recognize that we do not help members of disadvantaged groups by granting them entitlements or relaxing standards of evaluation; if we do, we only entrench them in their unequal status.

- Reconsider our teaching methods and curriculum and, where suitable, adapt them to the cultural requirements of our changing student body.
- Reconsider our employment procedures (including advertisement and interviewing methods) and, where suitable, change them to permit female and minority applicants to demonstrate their ability without having to leap needless hurdles.
- Establish incentives to encourage faculty and staff to seek greater responsibilities and more challenging assignments, regardless of paper qualifications. Where suitable, supply in-service training to assist such persons.
- Encourage intercultural communication between College members and the minority groups we serve (perhaps most notably Native Indians and recent immigrants), to identify problems and seek solutions acceptable to all without increasing our bureaucracy.
- Build stronger ties between the College and our region's high schools with a view to attracting women and minority group members—for example, by sending our female faculty to talk frankly with women students about career opportunities and requirements.
- Work closely with government agencies that support women (especially poor, single-parent, and battered women) and minority groups, to minimize barriers that keep members of those groups from enrolling in College programs. Lobby the government aggressively to fund enrollments and support services for members of such groups.
- Develop Intercultural Studies programs (not just Women's Studies, which tend to ghettoize both their faculty and their students) that will—for example—foster scrutiny of the canonical Western curriculum in the light of Native, Asian, and other cultures. Such

programs might include institutes dedicated to the study of South Asia, East Asia, Latin America, and other Pacific Rim cultures. They would draw their students from members of those cultures as well as the general population.

- Establish a Competitiveness Committee made up of faculty, staff, and administration that would periodically report on the quality of the workplace and the classroom in comparison to other B.C. colleges and universities. If it appeared that the College was falling behind (for example, in the number of Native Indians graduated, or temporary faculty regularized), the Committee would bring the matter to the attention of the College and the public. If the College were ahead of the competition, we would of course modestly bring this fact to the public's attention also.

No doubt we could come up with many more ideas, all of which would make the College more accessible to disadvantaged persons, more supportive of them, and more genuinely equitable to all—without creating special-status students or faculty, and without compromising our mission to provide rigorous education to the community we serve.

We Canadians are at this moment engaged in a struggle to define ourselves—a struggle for our own soul. We may well choose to define ourselves as an uneasy collection of unequal collectives, enjoying privileges (or lacking them) not because of what we've done but because of who we happen to be—what group we happen to belong to. If so, we will be well on the way to developing a caste society.

In a caste society, we would define ourselves not by what we have in common but what makes us separate and different from other people. We would not have a Capilano College. We would have a Capilano Women's College; a Capilano Native College; a Capilano Chinese College; a Capilano Gay College; and so on, until we no longer had a community college—or a community—at all. We would enter the 21st century with a striking resemblance to the U.S. South, circa 1920, or South Africa circa 1960, and we would be telling ourselves we had progressed from the bad old days.

Many of us have given half our lifetimes to this College. We started here in the 1960s and 1970s with the belief that we could help make this a more enlightened, democratic, and egalitarian society. We have seen the impact Capilano College has made—that we have made—helping to transform this society for the better in countless ways, and opening doors for thousands and thousands of people. I hope we have not wasted our efforts.

I wrote the foregoing as a loyal bureaucrat, and I stand by it even as I call for the contraction of the bureaucracy. Discussing what ought to be is futile if we refuse to recognize what exists now. The present system, of which my college is part, demands credentialed faculty, documented hours of credit per course, and evaluation based on academic standards of literacy, research methods, and critical thinking. Those standards have, of course, nothing to do with most students' real aspirations; they are just the "sprinting" requirement which everyone must submit to. But adding equity to the system would only turn the present parody of scholarship into a full-blown travesty.

The Equity Committee at least attacked the idea of credentialism, though not as effectively as it might have. If colleges were not so enslaved to the universities, college faculty credentials would indeed depend on teaching skills and experience rather than irrelevant scholarship; at that point many women would certainly out-compete their male counterparts. But it won't happen as long as the universities make up all the rules to maximize their markets and thereby justify an ever-growing bureaucracy.

Academic Freedom as an Exercise in Self-Deception

Credentialism and equity are not the only problems that result from post-secondary hypertrophy. As credentialism has made post-secondary a gateway to some fantasy Utopia of prosperous equality, some people enter it like street people venturing into a gentlemen's club. They admire the decor and the amenities in the toilets, but they don't much feel like members. The furniture is uncomfortable. The menu in the dining room is hard to read and lists very unfamiliar dishes. The staff are polite, but isn't that a contemptuous sneer hiding behind the waiter's smile? Aren't the old established members at the next table muttering about the decline of club standards?

As a matter of fact the waiter is indeed sneering, and the old members are disgusted at having to admit street people to what used to be a very congenial group of like-minded people. The street people, however, really are vital to the club's continued existence. They have every right to demand that the club serve their needs as well as it served the old members'.

I described post-secondary as a rite of passage. For the last two centuries in North America, it has been a painful rite that few could even aspire to. It demanded skills and attitudes and knowledge that few could acquire; those few, however, could then step confidently into positions of economic and political power. The process was a little easier because college and university values harmonized closely with the values of the elite families who sent their sons and daughters. One might go across the country to university, but the culture there was recognizable. What's more, it was a supremely self-confident culture.

Beginning with the rapid expansion of post-secondary after the Second World War, the culture began to change. Veterans came onto campus, deeply uninterested in the folkways of upper-class adolescent boys. A decade later, the middle class and working class were enrolling their children. They came out of vigorous cultures with little reason to adopt the values of their betters. Education was to get a better, more secure job, and not merely to acquire a veneer of literacy and some useful social connections.

By the 1970s, yet more groups were coming onto campus: blacks, immigrants, Native Indians, high-school dropouts, single parents, and others who would never have dreamed of post-secondary until now. They ran into trouble, just as a graduate of a Don Mills high school would have trouble at the Guangzhou Institute of Foreign Languages; the cultures were wildly different, and neither side felt ready to change.

The newcomers, of course, were at a severe disadvantage. The profs could simply carry on as they always had, and if the newcomers didn't get it they were soon gone. Maybe it looked bad if so many minorities did so poorly, but too bad—this was serious academic study and everyone had to measure up to the standard.

By the late 1980s, the minorities were no longer accepting this attitude; neither were many of the professors. The professoriat itself was now largely composed of the middle-class kids who'd filtered into the system in the 1950s and '60s. They had taken criticism themselves, in the wake of Sputnik, as scholastically hopeless. But both they and their critics shared the confident vision, taking for granted that enough knowledge, applied to any problem, must produce a solution. Their own education served them fairly well, after all, and provided many with an entry into professions formerly closed to them. Education ought to be able to do the same for blacks, Hispanics, and other historically marginalized groups.

Youths from these groups, however, displayed a striking mix of cockiness and insecurity. They expected to do well, and got defensive when they didn't. Many had grown up in a culture of victimism, not of elitism, and saw insults in everything from the skin colour of their English teachers to the content of the teachers' reading list.

Probably all students have felt angry and frustrated by the process of higher education. The children of the baby boomers, however, were not just students; they were *customers*, with customers' sovereign right to complain about bad service. The aging professors who provoked the complaints were easy targets. They were decent people who wanted to do the right thing for students with virtually no experience in scholarship or academic values. So they yielded to many of the minorities' points, and in the process harmed both the minorities and themselves.

A college education is supposed to be an upsetting, challenging experience that makes young people re-examine their own ideas; now, anything upsetting was by definition "offensive" and therefore unacceptable. I've already touched on such issues as the literary "canon" and the felt need to make literature more representative of the people who study it. That was the least of it.

In the United States, black students segregate themselves in "theme dorms" and "historically black" colleges try to stay that way. Chicano students go on hunger strikes to ensure that their own culture will enjoy affirmation as part of the bureaucratized academy. A department of Chicano studies makes them a legitimate contender in the fight for budgets and office space.

In both the U.S. and Canada, students shout down and harass professors who express unwelcome opinions. Whole fields of discussion—racial and sexual relations, the history of particular ethnic groups—have become off limits. No sensible professor will raise them because they will lead to protests, appearances before campus committees, and general harassment. In the 1950s, suspected Marxist sympathies could cost a professor his job; in the 1990s, mere bad manners are enough.

Bear in mind that this is happening in an institution that

loudly espouses academic freedom as the necessary condition for inquiry and debate. Moreover, because unpopular
opinions have cost many professors their jobs (and sometimes their lives), universities grant tenure to most faculty
who show they are competent scholars and teachers. Once
tenured, professors have a job for life unless they commit
serious crimes or their universities run into major financial
trouble.

By the mid-1990s, neither tenure nor academic freedom
was serving its intended purpose. In the overwhelming majority of disciplines, young scholars watch what they say
very carefully. An unacceptable opinion on, say, the nature
of dark matter, or the role of stomach bacteria in ulcer
formation, may endanger your career. But even if you got
tenure though your colleagues considered you "unsound,"
no one would really care outside your own narrow field.
Only in a handful of disciplines is anyone likely to become
unacceptable to society in general: sociology, political science, arts, economics.

In those cases, as several academics have learned to their
sorrow in recent years, tenure is no protection. Students
will either boycott your classes or take them over. The
media will swarm you, making research and teaching impossible. The university administration will rumble unhap-
pily; grants will dry up; journals will decline your work.
Your chief educational function will now be to serve as an
awful example of what happens when people step out of
line with the current orthodoxy.

Meanwhile, in less controversial disciplines, tenure
serves largely to protect coasters, incompetents, and charlatans. Their capable colleagues don't need tenure; chances
are that they're hopping from one university to another on
the strength of their burgeoning successes. But the less
able, once tenured, can blight the educations and careers
of hundreds of students. The administration knows intervention is always unpleasantly disruptive and only some-

times successful, so it rarely acts. Often (as in the public schools) the only tactful way to neutralize a bad professor is to invite him into the administration. This does not help improve administration, but at least it may open up a job for a better teacher and scholar.

I raise these embarrassing matters to argue that we can probably serve scholarship better by abandoning tenure than by maintaining it. Even the most experienced academics ought to be ready to defend their achievements every few years. They should also be ready to suffer dismissal or demotion if their peers find them inadequate.

Any untenured academic knows you've got to work like hell to keep your job. As a result, untenured faculty generally do good work both in their disciplines and in the housekeeping of their universities and colleges. So do most tenured faculty, but not all—and that small minority does a great deal of harm to the whole system. So dispensing with tenure would not affect the performance of most faculty, who would continue to work hard and well; but it would enable us to get rid of the academic racketeers.

What about academic freedom? How do we protect intellectual liberty if scholars lack job security? Pretty simply, I think. Universities and colleges simply state that their faculty and students, under the Charter of Rights and Freedoms, can say anything they like this side of libel and hate propaganda. Mere offensiveness would be no grounds for punishment; in fact, any attempt to silence participants in a debate (rather than refute them) would itself be grounds for disciplinary action.

Remember that I am offering a strategy for a fighting retreat of the education bureaucracy. My proposed defence of free speech would likely fail under the sheer political pressure that large groups of students can generate if they have the backing of parts of the public. Ultimately, this is a question we cannot answer but only beg. Not until universities escape from the credentialist treadmill and become much smaller groups of serious scholars will they enjoy real freedom of expression and inquiry. And when that happens, colleges in turn will be free to teach more freely also.

9

Bad Futures

Schools and society support one another in countless ways, each reinforcing or weakening some attitude or value in the other. School advocates tend to seek confident-vision solutions through social change: make the parents more concerned and the kids will study harder. Cautious-vision advocates argue the reverse: make the students work harder and society will be safer and richer. These opposing viewpoints lead to some predictable arguments that we should pause to consider. I don't think they'll really work, but many school-reform proposals include them.

The Magic Wand
This is the confident-vision strategy preferred by most people in the system. We might also call it hyperfunding. It sees nothing wrong with the basic system except a fuel shortage. If only we have enough money to deal with the problems we face, the problems are soluble.

So bright kids are bored? Spend money on enrichment programs to keep them challenged. So learning-disabled kids are struggling? Build and staff special learning centers.

So old schools are vulnerable to potential earthquakes? Retrofit them. Poor kids are coming to school hungry? Start up meal programs. And so it goes.

No doubt schools were cheaper thirty years ago in part because we neglected many children's needs and ducked genuine problems. We are doing a better job now, for more children, because we recognize those needs and try to address them. But the only certain outcome of hyperfunding is the generation of jobs in the bureaucracy. We may or may not actually help a specific learning-disabled child; we assuredly have people on the payroll. They, in turn, become part of government's concerns: they are consumers, taxpayers, contributors to retirement funds, part of someone's power base.

Up to a point this is acceptable. But if the solution to the problems of democracy is more democracy, the same is not true of bureaucracy's problems. The more it grows, the more it becomes its own reason for existence.

Worse yet, bureaucracy usually places itself in the role of patron, not servant. In ancient Rome, powerful men attracted hangers-on; in exchange for small handouts and the patron's influence, the hangers-on supplied entourages and voted the patron's way in elections. The name for such people was "clients"; modern bureaucracy uses the same term, because it always sees clients as intrinsically inferior people who can't look after themselves properly. That attitude is deeply hostile to the kind of education for freedom that I am proposing here, but it is entrenched in many forms of the confident vision. It wants to make everyone equal except those who decide how to impose equality on the rest of us.

The implicit assumption behind hyperfunding is that the schools will always find more and more people who can't look after themselves without the help of highly educated (or at least highly credentialed) specialists. Even if hyper-

funding fails to educate everyone to some desired level, it
succeeds: the failures only indicate the need to spend still
more.

Politically and financially, hyperfunding is out of the
question. We simply do not have the wealth, never mind
the desire, to pour money into a bottomless pit. Pedagog-
ically, hyperfunding is subversive of real educational goals
because it casts students in perpetually dependent roles: the
money, after all, would go to hire more credentialed ex-
perts to look after every possible real and imagined student
problem. Students would never escape clienthood; if they
tried, that would only be cause for hiring specialists in
"attitude deficiency disorder."

Back to Basics

Those who advocate this cautious-vision strategy conveniently forget that the basics they learned were in fact just
the current political response to public unhappiness with
education a generation ago. But if basics means strong emphasis on verbal skills (reading, writing, speaking, listening)
and numeracy, it has much to commend it.

As Harvard psychologist Howard Gardner has argued,
however, human beings possess at least seven different
kinds of intelligence; the verbal and mathematical forms
are highly important, but not all of us possess them in
equal measure. Similarly, not all of us possess musical intelligence, or the kind of physical intelligence that makes
some people great athletes or dancers. Moreover, we don't
always recognize those intelligences in children until we
expose them to challenges and opportunities.

So attention to verbal and mathematical skills will enable
some children to flourish while others achieve very little—
just as the current neglect of the performing arts means
some students' talents will atrophy from lack of exercise.

Even if we did adopt a back-to-basics curriculum, we
would have to diversify it. This would not be the kind of

streaming that most people of my generation endured, but a recognition that children coming from different backgrounds and experiences will gain verbal and mathematical skills in different ways. In some cases, rote learning works well; in others, it fails miserably. Self-paced learning works well with some students and horribly with others. One teacher's sure-fire gimmick may backfire badly in another teacher's classroom.

We could, at huge expense, force-march most children into greater basic literacy and numeracy. But the very emphasis we would have to place on basics would downgrade other skills and talents which might serve some children very well indeed. And while we could achieve such a triumph of training (know how) and schooling (know that), every student who stopped reading and writing after leaving school would be a failure of education (know why).

A more aggressive form of back-to-basics might be sheer elitism: at every opportunity, schools would test, stream and flunk until only a tiny cadre of top students (like some of my Columbia applicants) survived. This would save a great deal of money; we would need plenty of elementary teachers but only a few at the high school level and hardly any in post-secondary. It would also create a system reassuringly like what we suppose Oxford 1925 to have been, with young geniuses developing their talents under the close guidance of equally brilliant professors. Such a system would be a kind of intellectual eugenics, with the best and brightest selecting those yet better and brighter.

I would have more sympathy with this system if I had not taught in it. After the end of the Cultural Revolution, China restored the examination system. While it still made allowances for "equity" (less able rural students could get into post-secondary despite poorer test scores than their urban classmates), the Chinese system worked very well at identifying the brightest and most talented young people in the country.

Depending on their grades and test scores, Chinese students qualify for admission to top universities, less prestigious universities, or specialized training schools. Taken altogether, post-secondary students make up probably less than one percent of their age cohort. My students, at the Guangzhou Institute of Foreign Languages, considered themselves second- or third-raters because they had not gained admission to any of the "key" universities like Zhongshan—our crosstown rivals. Nevertheless, most were breathtakingly smart, highly motivated, and a joy to teach.

However, their political superiors cared very little for these carefully selected young people. Having identified an intellectual elite, the Chinese government was throwing it away in pointless, unrewarding jobs like tour guiding and translation of ceramics formulas. My students were smart enough to see what was going on, and remarkable numbers of them used their brains to get themselves out of the country for good. Many are now contributing to Canada's economy and education system.

By the same token, if we adopt an elitist education system we had better be prepared to give every graduate a prime job; otherwise, we will have trained our best young people for the benefit of some other country, or wasted our investment altogether. The elite had also better be smart enough to find productive work for the less bright, or the system will soon grind to a halt. And, ironically, the elite is likely to develop a confident vision directly opposed to the cautious ideology that created the elite in the first place.

Perestroika

"Restructuring" is a common occupation of bureaucrats who find flow charts more manageable than reality. Just as Gorbachev thought he could save communism by shaking up his bureaucracy, we like to imagine that the schools will recover if only we eliminate wasteful agencies, trim budgets, and oblige bureaucrats to work lean and mean. (The cliché betrays the shallowness of this insight.)

A typical restructuring idea is the longer school year. Many education critics point to the Japanese and some European systems in which students are in school for longer days, longer weeks, and longer terms. It might well work in some cases to improve test scores and reduce time spent on review. But its success would depend on a host of factors, not all of them under educator control.

For example, we would have to be certain that our course content and teaching style harmonize with a longer period of study. Doing the wrong thing, only doing it longer, would get us nowhere. We would have to ensure that quicker students met continuing challenges while slower ones weren't overwhelmed.

We would also have to resist the strong demand (strange in a free-enterprise nation) for the schools to take over yet more of the parenting role. A longer school day would minimize the loneliness of latchkey kids by keeping them at school until later in the afternoon. But it would also reinforce many parents' idea of school as babysitting service.

The long summer holiday is so ingrained that many parents would resent the inconvenience of having their children in school during the time when the family usually goes on holiday. Some might well just pull their children out for a couple of weeks, regardless of the impact on their schooling; plenty of parents do so already.

Since public opinion is so strongly against additional school spending, we would also have to find a way to teach longer at no further cost. Even if teachers and staff agreed to work longer for the same pay, we would have to pay more to keep schools warm on cold winter Saturdays and cool on hot July days. (Major maintenance and construction projects would be harder to manage without a long summer break also.)

Other restructuring ideas include reducing the numbers

of school districts (and thereby the number of trustees, senior administrators, central office staff, and so on); reducing the number of elective courses (and thereby the number of teachers); recruiting foreign students who will pay the full cost of their high-school education and thereby subsidize their classmates. Simple household economies also come in: closing underpopulated schools and selling the land, for example.

To an extent, restructuring can indeed work, just as reducing auto emissions by five percent is a feasible goal. But if that's all you do, a five percent increase in cars puts you back where you started. And if restructuring is purely cosmetic (as it usually is), the bureaucrats quickly become cynical masters of the game of musical chairs.

Just as computers have started to eliminate middle managers in business, they may well eliminate some levels of school administration. Government will then be able to deal directly with local schools just as some executives practice management by walking around on the shop floor. This could save some money, but not enough to save programs.

To succeed, restructuring ought to operate over the long term, as a response to a careful plan. More often it's a slapdash affair driven by last month's opinion poll and unlikely to make the bureaucracy smaller, more effective or more efficient. We have only to look at the private sector, whose bureaucracy is equally obtuse; there, management and stockholders are forever pursuing new fads and gurus who promise higher productivity and lower costs.

Privatism

Another alternative is the "privatist" school, which equips students to pursue their own interests without regard to social concerns. This is a very attractive concept to many people because it matches the ego-state values of the anticulture.

Privatism inspires some, but not all, of the push toward private education. Many parents prefer private schools because they feel their children will benefit from higher academic standards, more rigorous discipline, and a conventional curriculum. They are often right, and for the right reasons: such schooling may well increase their children's freedom as adults, and not merely their after-tax income. Other parents demand a religious content to their children's education precisely to equip them for adult responsibility within their religious community. As a result of such attitudes, private-school enrollments by the early 1990s reached an estimated 250,000 across Canada—almost five per cent of the total student population.

But many parents want only the blessings of self-aggrandizement for their children, and see private education as the best means to that end. Some religious families turn their backs on the larger society, and seek to close off their children from it as well.

Whether secular or religious, such privatism is a tempting alternative. It exempts us from confronting the dreadful problems we face as communities, as provinces, and as a nation among other nations. It encourages us to wait for a messiah, political or divine, and in the meantime to tolerate misery that we probably couldn't do much about anyway.

The larger society in most cases has to respect these privatist attitudes. But we are under no obligation to subsidize them, though many privatists think otherwise. That is where the famous voucher intrudes into education debates.

Voucherism calls for giving each household a kind of cheque for each child's yearly tuition, cashable at the school of the parents' choice. Normally the voucher is for whatever the average annual cost per pupil may be in the district. Parents can use it to enroll their child in any school they like—the local public school, or a private school across town. By analogy with free markets, vouchers should improve the quality of education by breaking the state monopoly. Schools that offer what parents want will flourish; bad schools will soon close for lack of pupils.

While free-enterprisers often endorse vouchers, the whole idea relies heavily on massive state subsidy and the continuation of bureaucratic education. Voucherism accepts that schools will continue to be costly, labour-intensive enterprises that no one can afford without public assistance. Amazingly, voucherists expect the taxpayers to donate more than $6,000 a year per child without anyone overseeing the process on the taxpayers' behalf.

Voucherism also assumes (as a cautious-vision idea) that parents understand what their children's educational needs are, and are prepared to seek out the best school to meet those needs. And it assumes that parents will have the time, experience, and resources to evaluate various schools and choose the most suitable. Doubtless some will, but a great many will not. They will plunk their kids down in the most convenient school (probably one within walking distance), without regard for the school's philosophy, teaching methods, assessment techniques, or anything else. Far from rewarding good schools, such parents could well sustain mediocrity or worse as long as it's within easy walking distance. (This of course is a confident-vision, teacher-knows-best attitude; the cautious vision would accept some parental mistakes as a worthwhile tradeoff for generally improved schools.)

Proponents of vouchers also overlook a couple of other problems. Six thousand dollars a year might be the average operating-budget cost per pupil, but many students will need much more. A special-needs child may well require a full-time aide whose salary would run to $25,000 a year or more, plus other specialists, plus extra equipment, and learning materials. A rural child will cost more just to transport and shelter, never mind actual teaching costs. Someone, therefore—a bureaucrat—will have to decide which children deserve extra money and which don't.

Those are only operating costs; capital costs don't come into the picture for voucherists. Suppose some brilliant band of teachers founds a new school. Who's going to pay for their building, their library, their computers? Do they expect taxpayers to donate some convenient building for the private benefit of the new school? And a well-capitalized school could undercut its competition by cleverly irrelevant marketing (pastel chalkboards! high-tech work stations! catered lunches!).

Every school that failed (and many have, in districts like Milwaukee that have experimented with vouchers) would not only be a waste of money and effort, but would compromise the education of its stranded students. Nor is it clear how unhappy parents could switch in mid-year; could they demand a pro-rata refund and march off to the school across the street? What if one bad teacher provoked a mass defection, ruining the work of a dozen others and threatening the school's existence?

Consider also a student who does poorly, and who turns out to have a problem the school can't deal with—attention deficit, perhaps. Does the school actually give up the student and her $6,000, or does it create its own attention-deficit program in hopes of squeezing more money out of the government? And will its program really work, or simply waste everyone's time? How will anyone tell? If the school must now sustain an attention-deficit expert in its bureaucracy, will that dilute its original purpose?

A problem for many people, though not for all, is that voucherism permits taxpayer support of religion. This is the present case in many jurisdictions already, but that doesn't mean it's a good thing. At least today's tax-subsidized religious schools must accept some degree of government supervision of their curriculum and standards. Vouchers would permit every church (and cult) to dip into tax money to indoctrinate children in its particular view of the world without much effective public influence.

Voucherism's persistence reflects a continuing parental alienation from the school system, a sense of powerlessness to influence children's education and therefore to be in charge of one's own life. That alienation is itself a powerful inducement to privatism and the rejection of democracy.

Despite the recession and our constitutional troubles, Canadians have remained notably tranquil. So have the Americans despite their own recession, despite their drug problems and their homeless and their violence in the streets. In striking contrast to the 1930s, no one is staging massive public protests about the public crisis in Canada or the U.S., because the dominant faith in North America these days is a cautious-vision belief in private salvation—that the world may go to hell but I can still get along very nicely, thank you. Despite all the evidence to the contrary, many of our students hope to do just that.

For all our professions of faith in the confident vision, we educators are often secret sharers of that belief in private salvation; we like to pretend, for example, that no matter what happens, we can still just close our doors and teach our kids as if nothing had changed. If we're honest we know that eventually we won't be able to do our jobs at all, but we console ourselves that maybe we'll be able to retire before it gets to that, or we'll win the lottery and quit.

I mentioned the "loyal insurgency" as a kind of social insurance policy, a way for a society to respond to unavoidable change. That privatist attitude is precisely what a loyal insurgency wants to attack and overthrow and discredit. An effective school system should make it clear to educators and students alike that we have no private salvation outside a healthy democratic society. We cannot allow our students to leave school thinking that they're okay because the leak isn't in their end of the lifeboat.

In other words, an effective school system must produce citizens in the classic sense of the word—people who take responsibility for governing their society. Those who fail to take responsibility cannot be considered educated. The Greeks had a word for such people, those who were entirely concerned with private affairs. The word was *idiot*.

10

Better Futures

The voucher idea has both practical and pedagogical problems in today's public-school context, but it's not absolutely wrong. We use a form of it already in colleges and universities, which receive government funding for each student they enroll. So if a student in Surrey, B.C., chooses to apply to North Vancouver's Capilano College instead of a local college like Douglas, the money goes to Capilano. (Unfortunately, the government puts a cap on the total number it will pay for, or we would be in hyperfunding heaven.) Vouchers also offer the promise of real diversity in the system.

One of the major problems I see with the standard voucher idea is that it gives public money to private individuals without much public control. If we could maintain such control, and we stopped fretting about "equal" education, we could offer some highly attractive options to parents and students.

The Virtual School
The depression of the 1930s radicalized the workers; the recession of the 1990s has radicalized the managers. Corporate bosses are revolutionizing their own organizations.

Top corporations like IBM and General Motors have grown too big and bureaucratic. Now they're cutting prices and laying off thousands in a desperate attempt to stay alive and competitive. In some cases managers are "re-engineering" their organizations, creating "virtual corporations"—temporary companies made up of small specialist firms that click together and come apart like Lego blocks.

In the public sector, meanwhile, education costs are far too high, the school bureaucracy absorbs too much money and energy, and results are not what they should be. Could we re-engineer a virtual school system? Here's one way it could work:

An educator proposes to her school board that she take over one of its schools and run it by a particular philosophy—conservative, liberal, experimental, whatever. She may be a teacher, a principal, a parent, an entrepreneur. She may have a PHD or no academic credentials at all. The important thing about her is that she has a coherent, attainable goal and demonstrable education-management skills. Her proposal shows that she's done her homework in a number of key areas:

- She's found that a reasonable number of parents and employers support her philosophy and teaching methods. She has a market for her services.
- Both employers and other education institutions are ready to accept students trained under this system: graduates should be able to earn both the Certificate of Basic Competency and admission to post-secondary. She has a market for her graduates.
- A number of teachers (not necessarily credentialed but demonstrably capable) are willing to work within her philosophy and conditions of employment.
- She can achieve her goals within existing budgets, and if she can achieve them for less than the board gives her, the balance will go into improving learning resources.

The board, if it likes her proposal, will fund her on a regular per-pupil basis, with bonuses for good student test scores (set by the province) and success rates (defined as attainment of specific skills and knowledge within a reasonable period of time).

As principal of her school, the educator hires her own staff, buys (or rents) her own equipment, and develops her own curriculum in line with general provincial standards. The curriculum may be comprehensive or specialized: perhaps the school wants to focus on math and science for girls, or on the B.C. Intermediate Program, or on running Advanced Placement and International Baccalaureate programs. If the school succeeds in attracting and holding students, and they perform as promised, it survives. If enrollments fall or students do poorly, the school board pulls the plug.

Whatever the school's philosophy, it doesn't measure education by hours of classroom time. Most real learning takes place in the time it takes to say "Aha!" So the school is constantly trying to move students along at their highest manageable pace. In effect, the principal is aiming at more "Ahas!" per dollar spent. If she can get a student through a year's study in six months, she's saved half of that student's funding. The unspent money can go into continuing the student's progress, plus extra help for slower students, buying new equipment, or whatever else will enhance the school's effectiveness. If she takes longer, her school pays for the extra time slower students require.

The school doesn't measure education by credentials or years of experience either. Teachers would work on individual, short-term contracts. Good student performance would mean bonuses and contract renewal. Poor performance would mean non-renewal, regardless of degrees held or seniority.

This need not mean sweatshop working conditions.

Teachers could form their own specialist consulting firms and offer their services to our hypothetical principal just as, say, lawyers now offer services to companies. One teaching firm might specialize in physical education, another in mathematics. As long as they got good results, such firms would prosper.

Both the school and its employees would have strong incentives to do the most with the least. Those who tried to make too much money would soon price themselves out of a job. Yes, it would be extremely insecure for many educators (especially the principals). They would be under intense competitive pressure, and the new system might not prevent individual abuses and even outright school bankruptcy. But serious educators could get on with serious teaching. Instead of being passive employees of a huge bureaucracy, they would be active partners with a stake in the success of their enterprise. They might even teach the corporate bureaucrats something about how to run a business.

Under this model, school boards could fund any school within their district—public, private, or in between. They could even fund the non-religious component of religious schools. Parents wishing to home-school could also ask for support and often receive it. Trustees could demand certain basic requirements: size and safety of classroom space, sanitation, and so on. They would closely monitor attendance, student progress, and teacher performance; if anything went wrong, the board would intervene promptly.

For some kinds of schooling, boards (or the provincial government) might pay extra. For example, emotionally disturbed children often demand much more attention than less troubled students, and may seriously disrupt classroom activities. A school willing to provide adequate facilities and staff qualified to deal with such students would receive extra funding. Some schools might accept only disturbed or disabled children while others continued to mainstream them; that would be a matter for the board, the school, and the parents to decide.

Such a regime would probably support a large number of fairly orthodox schools like those we have today. That's because most parents and students are pretty happy with standard chalk-and-talk teaching. But where teachers and parents were willing to try something different, the opportunity would be there. Virtual schools might occupy a single classroom, one small school building, or several sites—including shopping malls, office towers, or any other useful venue.

So if parents wanted a fairly structured, highly academic school, they could have it. If they wanted something loose and child-centered, they could have that too.

This approach may seem subversive to you; let me spell out some of its greatest horrors.

The school is not egalitarian or universal. One of the great disasters of modern public education, as Theodore Sizer observes in his book *Horace's Compromise*, is that if something works well for some students, we impose it on all students. Then we have the gall to consider this imposition a recognition of students' right to equal schooling. As a result, surveys of North American education reveal an astonishing sameness in schools, whether they serve affluent middle-class whites or destitute blacks, inner-city kids or rural kids. For all our fashionable talk of child-centered education, as educators we think mostly about how to inveigle students (whatever their background) into accepting and learning the same basic facts, skills, and attitudes through the same basic methods.

More important than equal schooling is the opportunity to enter adult life on an equal footing with others. If a principal can persuade her board that she can do a better job with learning-disabled children, or gifted children, or immigrants, she can set the terms of admission: a particular test score, a long interview, a contractual agreement with the student.

She may argue that girls learn math and science better when they're not in class with boys; so she can segregate her students by sex if she likes. The onus is then on her to send her students on with math and science skills equal (or superior) to those of students in unsegregated schools. Or she may demand a high entrance-exam score before admitting students to an Advanced Placement program, having guaranteed her board that her graduates will indeed qualify for Advanced Placement when they enter post-secondary. No results, no school next year.

This method raises the specter of racial and ethnic segregation as well. Suppose a group of Native Indian teachers want to start a Natives-only school, an enclave with Coast Salish or Mohawk as the language of instruction. Suppose some expatriate Britons want their own ethnic enclave, something like a British public school complete with headmaster. A board could approve both schools, with a major proviso: graduates of each school must demonstrate good understanding of the cultural values and experiences of students in other schools.

We do not force peanut-butter sandwiches on children with serious allergies to peanuts, and we should not force particular cultural values on children that put them in a double bind. Despite decades of domination by the confident vision, public education has disastrously failed millions of children who happen to be black, Native Indian, or otherwise culturally out of step with the larger society. False egalitarianism has aggravated the problem it set out to solve, and after the past half-century we should be ready to try new approaches.

Do not misunderstand me. I am not calling for a return to Jim Crow, and I am not contradicting my own argument for a democratic school system that trains citizens. If an "enclave" school can equip its students only for life in an ethnic ghetto, the school doesn't deserve even to start. But if children can gain a solid education that gives them a confident sense of their own identity, they will have much more to contribute to everyone else.

Some may argue that such segregation would restrict students' social education, making them awkward and un-communicative with students from outside their own school. Most teachers today are wearily aware that racism and sexism flourish in many of our ostensibly non-racist, non-sexist schools: notice who sits with whom in the cafeteria, or hangs out with whom between classes. Remember that one required outcome of enclave schools would be familiarity with the cultures of other groups. In other words, students would have to study one another, really learn what was going on with those other kids.

In any case, not many schools would rely on such segregation; most would doubtless be open to all. A Coast Salish school could welcome non-Native children; a school for the physically disabled could still admit able-bodied children. The educational benefits would surely be great for all concerned.

But segregation would be only one potential horror for this kind of school. I mentioned that neither the principal nor her teachers need credentials. They are ready to stand or fall by their students' achievement, not by their possession of a teaching credential and an advanced degree. Their school's accreditation will likewise depend on student achievement.

This policy is a dagger at the throat of every university education department and every tenured professor within it. If uncredentialed teachers can find work, and do well, not many people will voluntarily apply to education school. Or if they do, they will demand training in the methods used by the most successful principals. (Many principals would doubtless run their own in-service training.)

Salaries and working conditions would vary dramatically

within a given school district, and perhaps even within a given school. Suppose a Montessori school is starting up with relatively low enrollments, and dedicated Montessori teachers really want it to succeed; they may work for low salaries to help get it going, knowing they'll receive a bonus if the students do well.

If teachers begin to see themselves as consultants on a performance-based contract instead of employees putting in time, they may prefer to move their students more quickly through the material. Then the teachers would be free to take on another contract that much sooner.

Now the dagger is at the throat of the teachers' union. Seniority is gone. Salary schedules based on credentials and length of service are gone. Working conditions are variable. Contracting out is the new standard. The principal, not the union or the College of Teachers, decides whom to hire and at what salary. (If she's wise, she at least consults with her current teachers as well as parents.) Her school survives at the pleasure of the parents and the trustees. If they shut it down, she and her teachers are out of work and in no position to bump anyone else out of a job. If teachers do indeed form consulting firms, their unemployed partners will have to hustle up new contracts wherever they can find them.

This would be a deeply distasteful prospect for many teachers; after all, they didn't go into education to become entrepreneurs, and they don't relish the idea of spending their whole careers in a state of insecurity. However, most schools would remain fairly orthodox. Principals and boards would be slow to set up a really offbeat kind of school unless they could see a strong demand for it; that demand would tend to ensure reasonable stability for the new school and its teachers.

As public schools, all such institutions would have to equip their students with some form of the core curriculum mentioned earlier. How they chose to do so would be their business. But the schools would accept some form of external examination to assess their achievement.

Who Drives the Schools?

Let's look at how the system might run early in the 21st century.

If public education is training for citizenship, then some kind of government body (independent of the government of the day) sets the standards for graduation and demands accountability. Meeting the standards involves a series of tests and presentation of a portfolio of work. Students take the tests whenever they feel ready, and if they fail some parts they return to school knowing where to focus their energies. Students are free, once they have their CBC, to leave school and seek work. Or they can remain in school to pursue further training for the job market.

Now the government steps out of the picture, since it has fulfilled its obligation to train citizens. Except as an employer itself, government has little to say about further worker training. Companies and professional bodies now set their own entrance exams for applicants, and they can set them to whatever standard they consider realistic and appropriate for entry-level workers. The requirements are detailed and specific, so that students understand what they have to master.

Where they master the requirements doesn't matter much. Some job training happens within the public schools; other programs run in the community colleges and universities; still others flourish in private schools and through independent self-paced learning. Most programs deliver much of their material online or on some form of CD-ROM; creating effective materials for these media has become a major industry in itself. Curriculum goes through versions, like software applications, as experience reveals unexpected weaknesses and the authors respond with upgrades.

Some employers run their own entrance exams and

maybe their own training programs; others designate particular courses and programs available in the area or through online services. Any applicant can challenge an employer's entrance exam, regardless of previous education. And no previous education exempts an applicant from the entrance exam; mere possession of a bachelor's degree, as we are learning in the 1990s, is no guarantee even of basic literacy.

This approach has a liberating effect on public schools and colleges: it frees them from the demands of universities. The universities now are just another set of employers, and they are free to set their own entrance exams and job requirements, but they can no longer dictate the terms of education for people seeking careers elsewhere. They can tell an aspiring professor that she must take this or that course, but employers and professionals define the education they want in their own recruits.

Without an ever-growing captive market, Canadian universities have found out who really loves them. They have also learned that less is more. Their focus is on research and publication, with teaching as a minor activity for training apprentice scholars. The number of faculty they need is a fraction of the 38,000 working in the early 1990s; this is just as well, since the mass retirements at the turn of the century would otherwise have posed a hideous recruitment problem.

By heavy attrition and the abandonment of tenure, universities have regained their status as places of first-rate scholarship and research. Empire-building is still possible (the small number of superb researchers has created a sellers' market in some disciplines), but is no longer a cost of doing business in advanced education.

What has happened to staff and faculty too young to retire? Many of them have gone into the private sector, or the burgeoning colleges. There, as in the public schools, an educator with a thoughtful proposal can find provincial,

regional or private venture capital to set up and run training programs.

The process in the 1990s was horribly slow and cum-
bersome, requiring long rumination by provincial bureaucrats; it was no way to respond to a rapidly changing job
market. Now, a specialized job-training program can qualify students within weeks or months—and when the market
demand ceases, the program vanishes or mutates.

An Interim Measure: The Summer Institute

This scaled-down post-secondary system would obviously
take years to establish; in the meantime, we owe the students and teachers in the present system some way to cope.
One stopgap would be to enhance the current funding formula with cost-recoverable credit courses.

Canada's colleges and universities, for the foreseeable
future, will probably get budgets with zero for inflation.
That means a major shortfall every year because the system
is locked into rising payments for invisible items like employee benefits. California shows us where we will end up.
Its post-secondary system, once the greatest in the world,
is collapsing under repeated annual budget cuts—up to ten
percent a year. That disaster will be upon us soon unless
we find a solution. The solution is partial privatization.

If post-secondary costs keep rising, demand for seats
keeps growing, and government refuses to keep pace, we
confront some serious problems. First, colleges and universities have ceased to accept any more students than the
government funds them for: If the budget funds, say, the
equivalent of 2,000 full-time students (FTE), then the door
closes in the face of student No. 2,001 and everyone else
in line.

To select students, schools tend to register previous enrolled students first, and then new students with high
grade-point averages. Those with relatively poor GPA's then
have a real problem. The later they register, the fewer

choices they have. Since they need at least three courses to qualify for a student loan, many late registrants desperately sign up for courses that mean nothing to them and won't advance their education plans. But if they get a decent grade (a gamble, given their poor academic record), they may at least be able to register earlier next semester. The whole system, while understandable, is grossly wasteful of everyone's time and energy.

Meanwhile, colleges and universities can't offer their temporary faculty enough steady work to keep them at a decent income level—despite the high student demand. The result is poor morale, administrative problems, and sometimes inappropriate assignments. Many temporary faculty, as desperate as their students, moonlight in different institutions and can't give their best effort anywhere.

A two-tier system could actually improve both access and post-secondary completion rates, maintaining and improving existing programs while offering adequate work to temporary faculty.

Most campuses are empty in summer because colleges can't afford to run courses then. They'd have to use some of their precious FTE funding, which would mean fewer places for students in the September onslaught. Even so, thousands can't get the courses they need and take whatever they can get. Thousands more can't handle full-time study. Predictably, many quit or flunk out.

Colleges could, however, offer far more summertime "cost-recoverable" credit courses than they do now. Students' tuition fees would cover the whole cost—instructors, administration, everything.

Students would indeed pay a premium for such "Summer Institute" courses, but not an outrageous one. A "section" is one semester-long, three-credit course; at most colleges, eight sections make a full-time annual workload. The cost of a section varies with the pay of the instructor, but most temporary faculty are near the bottom of the salary scale. Suppose it costs $8,000 to run a section—salary, benefits, administration, and marketing. If the section enrolls thirty students, the per-student cost would be $265. If Summer Institute tuition were $350 per section, that section would gross $10,500—and the college or university would gain a $2,500 profit. In fact, the section could enroll as few as twenty-three students and still break even. Students meanwhile would enjoy the best classrooms and labs on campus, with little competition for other resources.

Taking a couple of intensive eight-week courses would be easier for many students than trying to handle a full course load over fifteen weeks. Once through their summer courses, they could also choose a lighter, more manageable course load in the fall and spring. Or they could use their summers to prepare for full-time study. Either way, they'd have a better chance of completing their education rather than dropping out.

Many of the students would be academically less prepared than the average, but they would benefit from frequent student-teacher contact, especially in small-group tutorials and individual interviews. Faculty could identify those with serious problems and refer them to advisors well before the onset of the fall semester. In some cases, even those students who failed a Summer Institute course could take it again during the regular year without falling behind their classmates.

Cost-recoverable courses, offered on this basis, could dramatically reduce the pressure on September registration. Weak students, who normally have to register last, could jump the queue—for a price. So could good students who want to cram more courses into a year. Meanwhile colleges could offer more work for their faculty and staff than government money would permit. That would maintain quality, diversity, and flexibility.

Yes, this would be a two-tier system, with easier access for affluent students. But the present system, as California shows, simply can't survive. If we cut programs and classes, access for low-income students will only worsen. Cutbacks also mean a reduction in education quality: larger classes, fewer courses, less individual attention.

Traditional supporters of public education might say a two-tier system is unfair. Yet such a system would actually ensure the broad access they say they want—by creating a voluntary subsidy from rich users to help keep a first-rate system available to all.

The Student-Defined Program

Post-secondary educators are keenly aware that the job market is changing faster than they—and their political masters—can. By the time we and the bureaucrats have recognized an opportunity, years have passed; so has the opportunity. Many of us write proposal after proposal, outlining new training programs to meet such needs, but the proposals go nowhere.

One solution is to open up the present kind of career training, which obliges students to take a whole predetermined sequence of courses, and to let them major in a self-defined program. In some cases, such a program might enable students to take particular courses from a smorgasbord, and emerge with a toolkit of skills for an occupation too specialized and fast-changing for regular programs— without retooling curriculum, hiring new faculty, or creating still more bureaucracy.

Suppose, for example, a student wants to become a freelance book and periodical designer. She takes some courses in small business management (she's going to be a small business when she graduates), marketing, typography, mass media, graphics, communication theory, computers—all courses that already serve various groups of students. She "hitch-hikes" in these courses, which serve much larger career programs, so she doesn't add much to the administrative burden. She may be the only book and periodical designer her college produces in three years, and perhaps the only one the market can absorb. But she's out there, armed with the right skills, and it's cost her college virtually nothing to produce her.

Perhaps ideas like summer institutes, two-tier tuition, and self-designed programs sound far-fetched, but the only way out of a Catch-22 is to change the terms of the problem. Traditional post-secondary is a luxury we can no longer afford.

Paying the Bill

And what about funding for public education? There again we need some new ideas.

British Columbians have reason to remember the school-funding crunch of the early 1980s. The recession-plagued Socred government faced falling revenues and rising school costs. A real-estate boom made homeowners into helpless tax targets. The Socreds' answer was to dismantle locally controlled education. They took the commercial-industrial tax base away from school boards and folded it into the provincial share of funding. (This was to provide more "equality" for non-industrial districts. Or so they said.) If boards needed more money, they would have to take it out of their homeowners alone. Then boards, not the Socreds, would take the heat.

Later the Socreds took all taxing power away from school boards, putting trustees in an impossible bargaining position. The NDP opposition complained, but didn't change things once it gained power.

Funding the schools out of residential property taxes is easy to do but hard to justify. Homeowners of course get some benefit out of having good schools, but so does everyone else. The difference is that homeowners are sitting targets. Tax a corporation too hard and it moves to Mexico. Tax a home too hard and its owner can only sell to a more affluent victim.

And why should homeowners pay so unevenly? Ministry figures show that in twenty-one B.C. school districts the average property owner paid nothing for the schools in 1992. In fifty-four districts the taxpayer paid $152, and in Vancouver the amount was $390.

In the Maritimes, school budgets come entirely out of provincial funding. B.C. is moving in that direction too, but in the wrong way. While some of our property tax may supposedly be earmarked for the schools, in fact it all goes into general revenue and then goes into education or whatever else Victoria wants. In other words, it's like federal funding for colleges and hospitals. Ottawa may claim the money is for those purposes, but once the province gets the cheque it can spend it any way it likes, especially after Paul Martin's 1995 budget, which granted provinces the power to allocate federal transfer payments wherever the provinces wish.

What would work better? The answer looks like general provincial revenue, especially income taxes. Income is closely tied to education level attained, at least for middle-aged workers. So those who have gained the most from their education would contribute most to school funding. The poor would pay relatively little, and they wouldn't have to pay their landlords' school taxes indirectly through their rent.

The province could still ensure some local control by putting a percentage of spending in the hands of locally elected trustees. While the province handled major contract bargaining, local boards could make side deals for local conditions and provide venture capital for local programs—useful experience for future virtual schools. Teachers and staff might not like bargaining with the province, but that would reflect financial reality.

I wish I could offer a specific dollar saving for these ideas. But if it currently costs over $6,000 to keep a British Columbia teenager in school for a year, then in constant dollars we spend $72,000 to get him through twelve years. If we can get that teenager to graduation a year early, we can put the unspent $6,000 to use somewhere else—maybe in helping to keep a potential dropout in school long enough to graduate.

If we can get everyone through in ten years, we save the cost of two years' tuition—$12,000 per student. And if we had done that in B.C. in 1992-93, we would have saved the costs of schooling over 88,000 students (not counting those who dropped out). That would amount to just over a billion dollars.

Canadian universities awarded over 100,000 bachelor's degrees in 1989. If it costs $20,000 for every year of university, and if we had graduated those students in three years instead of four, we'd have saved two billion dollars. A billion here, a billion there . . . pretty soon, as the late U.S. Senator Everett Dirksen once observed, we're talking real money.

11

Schools for Chaos

At this point in the genre of the education-reform book, I should be offering a gorgeous vision of future schools. The buildings are clean, bright and airy; the teachers use some patented Secret Weapon to make everyone literate, numerate, polite, and employable. Education costs make no impact on taxpayers; teachers work happily for minimum wage; the textbooks are recent, packed with facts in entertaining form, and completely unoffensive; every student has a brand-new computer loaded with brilliant interactive software, donated by socially responsible private enterprise. All the parents are involved, and the schools jump to adopt every parental suggestion. Everyone loves everyone else and the only problem is prying the kids out of the classroom at the end of the day.

Schools for chaos would be far too diverse to suit such a vision. For every school using phonics as its Secret Weapon, another would be doing just as well with whole language—or some as yet unknown technique. For every school in a typical 1990s building, another would be operating in a parent's basement with nothing but a bulletin-board server and a fax machine; the kids would all be at home except for field trips, soccer games, and choir practice.

Some students would need fourteen years to achieve their Certificate of Basic Competency, and would take plenty of kidding about it; others would have the CBC after nine or ten years, get an entry-level job, and continue with school in the evenings or on weekends (or online). Employers would stop fretting about employee illiteracy and start wondering about the maturity levels of fourteen-year-olds who are otherwise qualified to hold jobs.

It would be impossible to point to a date on the calendar and say: "This was the day the Glorious Revolution began." The old bureaucratic system will survive for a long time. The awful thing about bureaucracies is that they work; they work even better when they're small enough to stay in touch with the people they serve.

Developing schools for chaos would be a matter not of upheaval but of erosion. As more students moved into virtual schools, and more teachers moved with them, the bureaucratic system would require less money and fewer people. (It would never admit that, of course, except in private.) Parents and children happy with orthodox schools would have every reason to stay with them. Those wanting something else could find it at a reasonable price.

For a long time, snobbery would be fierce on both sides. Universities, teachers' unions, and other vested interests would uphold credentialism as the one true purpose and yardstick of education. Supporters of virtual schools would laugh at them—as long as employers stuck to their guns and hired people on the basis of ability and not certification. Each side would harbour a secret envy of the other. In an odd reversal, the cautious-vision people would flock to virtual schools because such schools would offer real results; the confident-vision people would stick to orthodox credentialism with its ritualistic process of climbing up the grade ladder.

Each side would also discover weaknesses as erosion continued. Many university researchers would find they simply couldn't conduct the kind of big projects once feasible in the days of multi-billion-dollar budgets. Private fund-raising would become a chore as tedious as teaching ever was. Some departments might close down altogether because of lack of interest.

The public system would find that not every fast-talking educator with a laser-printed proposal was also a sound administrator with a valid philosophy. Some virtual schools would fail badly. Even the successful ones might operate, intentionally, for just a couple of years before closing down and turning themselves into something else. Teachers on contract might move from one district to another, not always at convenient times. Nothing would stay the same for long, and many people would find that frustrating.

But whatever methods provided success would offer guidelines to others. A Cree-immersion school that graduated all its students and sent half on to further education would inspire others to adopt its techniques—and not only Native Indian schools. A private college that graduated immigrants as fluent English speakers would generate plenty of imitators; maybe it would franchise itself.

In a strange way, the success of such a system would be hard for many people to take. A dog on a chain always disapproves of a dog who's not. Most of us have very little freedom in our lives, and we usually feel outrage at the trivial uses that the rich (and the adolescent) make of their freedom. Our schools would no longer be training new wage slaves for boring jobs, but educating free people for the often painful demands of citizenship. If educators do their job properly, and students leave school with no agenda but their own, we will often feel baffled and scandalized by what they choose to do.

I have no idea how people educated in schools for chaos would behave. They might all have a passionate hatred for calculus, or regard Canadian history as surpassingly dull. But at least they would be free to reject those subjects.

Northrop Frye once observed that you are not free to refuse to play the piano until you can play the piano. By
equipping all students with as much knowledge and as
many skills as possible, we could give them genuine
choices—better choices, in fact, than we ourselves have
had.

Yes, it will be hard to equip those kids for challenges
we can't foresee. Nevertheless, *our* teachers did make us
more complicated than we had been, and we have been
coping pretty well ever since with the built-in chaos of life.
I think we can do at least as well, if we take our work
seriously enough.

If we choose instead to give our scarce resources only
to the rich and powerful, our future is much more predictable: it will be very much like the worst parts of the past.
Orwell sums it up very well in *Nineteen Eighty-Four* when
his version of the Grand Inquisitor, O'Brien, tells Winston
Smith: "If you want a vision of the future, imagine a boot
stamping on a human face—forever."

All that is required for the triumph of that kind of evil
is for good teachers to do nothing. Even if educators do
act positively to create a worthwhile future, they still have
no guarantee that they will win. Those who hold the confident vision might reflect on what confidence has achieved
(and failed to achieve) in its decades of dominating public
education. Those who hold the cautious vision might reflect on the fate of those who have failed to learn in the
face of the unpredictable—including both themselves and
their confident fellow-citizens.

If we parents and teachers do our job right, however,
our children will learn that learning makes them free—free
of the bullying of confident-vision bureaucrats and free of
the dead hand of cautious-vision orthodoxy. If we do our
job wrong, our children will associate learning only with
failure and humiliation. If they accept that poisonous, can-
cerous lie, as so many of them seem to, then we have

betrayed not only them but ourselves and those of our students who do manage to succeed. If we throw away our children's lives, we throw away our own as well.

We don't know—we can't know—if we are creating a worthwhile future by what we do, or destroying it. All we can do is to struggle to understand ourselves, and then to convey that understanding to our children. If we sometimes wonder if it's worthwhile, if our students really do have a right to an education, perhaps we should think about the generations before us, whose faith and hope overcame their doubts and fears. They prepared us, whether they knew it or not, for the dazzling, frightening, hopeful chaos of today; we can do the same for our children.

Sources

Some of the information in this book comes from columns or articles I wrote some time ago, and whose sources are no longer immediately available. What follows, therefore, is only a partial list of the works I consulted.

Alberta. *Education in Alberta: Facts and Figures 1991*. Edmonton: Alberta Education, 1992.

British Columbia. "Improving the Quality of Education in British Columbia: Changes to British Columbia's Education Policy." Victoria: Ministry of Education, 1993.

British Columbia. *A Legacy for Learners: The Report of the Royal Commission on Education*. Barry M. Sullivan, Commissioner. Victoria: Queen's Printer, 1988.

British Columbia. *British Columbia Population Forecast 1990–2016*. Ministry of Finance, 1991.

British Columbia. *A Precis of the Report of the Royal Commission on Education in British Columbia, 1960*. Dean S. F. Chant, Commissioner. Victoria: Queen's Printer, 1960.

British Columbia. Ministry of Education. *Annual Report* (1984–1992).

Brodeur, Paul. *The Great Power-Line Cover-Up*. Boston: Little, Brown, 1993.

Canada. Department of the Secretary of State. *Higher Education in Canada.* Alexander D. Gregor & Gilles Jasmin, editors. 1992.

Canada. Department of the Secretary of State. *Profile of Higher Education in Canada,* 1991 edition.

Colombo, J. R., ed. *The 1994 Canadian Global Almanac.* Toronto: Macmillan of Canada, 1993.

Economic Council of Canada. *A Lot to Learn: Education and Training in Canada.* Ottawa: Ministry of Supply & Services Canada, 1992.

Frye, Northrop. *On Education.* Toronto: Fitzhenry & Whiteside, 1988.

Gilder, George. "The Death of Telephony." *The Economist,* September 11, 1993, 75-78.

Kilian, Crawford. *School Wars: The Assault on B.C. Education.* Vancouver: New Star, 1985.

Lewington, Jennifer & Graham Orpwood. *Overdue Assignment: Taking Responsibility for Canada's Schools.* Toronto: John Wiley & Sons, 1993.

Neatby, Hilda. *So Little for the Mind: An Indictment of Canadian Education.* Toronto: Clarke, Irwin, 1953.

Perelman, Lewis J. *School's Out: Hyperlearning, the New Technology, and the End of Education.* New York: Morrow, 1992.

Picot, G. *The Changing Education Profile of Canadians, 1961 to 2000.* Treasury Board of Canada, 1980.

Projections of Elementary and Secondary Enrolment and the Teaching Force in Canada, 1987-88 to 2006-07. Canadian Teachers' Federation, 1989.

Sauvé, Roger. *Canadian People Patterns: What's in the Cards for You?* Saskatoon: Western Prairie Producer Books, 1990.

Sizer, Theodore R. *Horace's Compromise: The Dilemma of the American High School.* Boston: Houghton Mifflin, 1984.

Smith, Stuart. *Report: Commission on Inquiry on Canadian University Education.* Ottawa: Association of Universities and Colleges of Canada, 1991.

Sowell, Thomas. *A Conflict of Visions: Ideological Origins of Political Struggle.* New York: W. Morrow, 1987.

Teacher Supply and Demand in British Columbia to the Year 2011: Executive Summary. Victoria: Pacific Analytics, Inc. & Richmond: Strategic Concepts, Inc., 1993.

West, Edwin G., Caryn Duncan, and Jonathan R. Kesselman. *Ending the Squeeze on Universities.* Montreal: Institute for Research on Public Policy, 1993.

Wickstrom, Rod. "Images of the CEO: Reflections on Reality." In Vernon Storey, ed., *Perspectives on Leadership.* Toronto: Canadian Association of School Administrators, 1992.

Index

Justa / *Bridget Moran*
The moving biography of Justa Monk, former Triabl Chief of the Carrier Sekani Nation, who overcame great personal odds to become a respected leader of his people. *$14.95*

A Little Rebellion / *Bridget Moran*
The fiery autobiography of a social worker who rebelled against an official system that worked against those for whom it was designed. "An intensely personal account of one woman's private protest movement." —*Vancouver Sun* *$13.95*

The NESA Activities Handbooks
Native Educational Services Associates
Three volumes of educational activities for use in Native and multicultural classrooms. The activities stress the importance of culture in students' lives, and teaches them basic personal and community-related skills so they may become more self-reliant and culturally responsible. *Vol. 1: $12.95; Vols. 2 & 3: $14.95 each*

ARSENAL PULP PRESS titles are available through your favourite bookstore, or prepaid directly (add $2.50 per title for shipping, plus 7% GST in Canada only) from:

ARSENAL PULP PRESS
100-1062 Homer Street
Vancouver, BC Canada v6b 2w9

Write for a copy of our free catalogue.